THE KEY
STUDENT STUDY GUIDE

Science 9

W9-CPE-749

THE KEY student study guide is designed to help students achieve success in school. The content in each study guide is 100% curriculum aligned and serves as an excellent source of material for review and practice. To create this book, teachers, curriculum specialists, and assessment experts have worked closely to develop the instructional pieces that explain each of the key concepts for the course. The practice questions and sample tests have detailed solutions that show problem-solving methods, highlight concepts that are likely to be tested, and point out potential sources of errors. **THE KEY** is a complete guide to be used by students throughout the school year for reviewing and understanding course content, and to prepare for assessments.

Rao, Gautam, 1961 –
THE KEY – Science 9
    Alberta

    1. Science – Juvenile Literature. I. Title

Published by
Castle Rock Research Corp.
2340 Manulife Place
10180 – 101 Street
Edmonton, AB T5J 3S4

    4 5 6 FP 13 12 11

Publisher
Gautam Rao

Contributors
Colbie Bell
Ken Boyko
Alison English-Donner
Jeff Goldie
Ruby Grewal
Robin Hill
Selma Losic
Mithlesh Nandni Rehani
Earl Wolff

Dedicated to the memory of Dr. V. S. Rao

THE KEY—Science 9

THE KEY consists of the following sections:

KEY Tips for Being Successful at School gives examples of study and review strategies. It includes information about learning styles, study schedules, and note taking for test preparation.

Class Focus includes a unit on each area of the curriculum. Units are divided into sections, each focusing on one of the specific expectations, or main ideas, that students must learn about in that unit. Examples, definitions, and visuals help to explain each main idea. Practice questions on the main ideas are also included. At the end of each unit is a test on the important ideas covered. The practice questions and unit tests help students identify areas they know and those they need to study more. They can also be used as preparation for tests and quizzes. Most questions are of average difficulty, though some are easy and some are hard—the harder questions are called *Challenger Questions*. Each unit is prefaced by a ***Table of Correlations***, which correlates questions in the unit to the specific curriculum expectations. Answers and solutions are found at the end of each unit.

KEY Strategies for Success on Tests helps students get ready for tests. It shows students different types of questions they might see, word clues to look for when reading them, and hints for answering them.

Practice Tests includes one to three tests based on the entire course. They are very similar to the format and level of difficulty that students may encounter on final tests. In some regions, these tests may be reprinted versions of official tests, or reflect the same difficulty levels and formats as official versions. This gives students the chance to practice using real-world examples. Answers and complete solutions are provided at the end of the section.

For the complete curriculum document visit http://education.alberta.ca/teachers/program/science/programs.aspx

THE KEY *Study Guides* are available for many courses. Check www.castlerockresearch.com for a complete listing of books available for your area.

For information about any of our resources or services, please call Castle Rock Research at 780.448.9619 or visit our website at http://www.castlerockresearch.com.

At Castle Rock Research, we strive to produce an error-free resource. If you should find an error, please contact us so that future editions can be corrected.

TABLE OF CONTENTS

NOTES

KEY Tips for Being Successful at School

KEY TIPS FOR BEING SUCCESSFUL AT SCHOOL

KEY FACTORS CONTRIBUTING TO SCHOOL SUCCESS

In addition to learning the content of your courses, there are some other things that you can do to help you do your best at school. Some of these strategies are listed below.

- **Keep a positive attitude:** Always reflect on what you can already do and what you already know.

- **Be prepared to learn**: Have ready the necessary pencils, pens, notebooks, and other required materials for participating in class.

- **Complete all of your assignments:** Do your best to finish all of your assignments. Even if you know the material well, practice will reinforce your knowledge. If an assignment or question is difficult for you, work through it as far as you can so that your teacher can see exactly where you are having difficulty.

- **Set small goals for yourself when you are learning new material:** For example, when learning the parts of speech, do not try to learn everything in one night. Work on only one part or section each study session. When you have memorized one particular part of speech and understand it, then move on to another one, continue this process until you have memorized and learned all the parts of speech.

- **Review your classroom work regularly at home:** Review to be sure that you understand the material that you learned in class.

- **Ask your teacher for help**: Your teacher will help you if you do not understand something or if you are having a difficult time completing your assignments.

- **Get plenty of rest and exercise:** Concentrating in class is hard work. It is important to be well-rested and have time to relax and socialize with your friends. This helps you to keep your positive attitude about your school work.

- **Eat healthy meals:** A balanced diet keeps you healthy and gives you the energy that you need for studying at school and at home.

 # How To Find Your Learning Style

Every student learns differently. The manner in which you learn best is called your learning style. By knowing your learning style, you can increase your success at school. Most students use a combination of learning styles. Do you know what type of learner you are? Read the following descriptions. Which of these common learning styles do you use most often?

- **Linguistic Learner**: You may learn best by saying, hearing, and seeing words. You are probably really good at memorizing things such as dates, places, names, and facts. You may need **to write and then say out loud** the steps in a process, a formula, or the actions that lead up to a significant event.

- **Spatial Learner**: You may learn best by looking at and working with pictures. You are probably really good at puzzles, imagining things, and reading maps and charts. You may need to use strategies like **mind mapping and webbing** to organize your information and study notes.

- **Kinaesthetic Learner**: You may learn best by touching, moving, and figuring things out using manipulative. You are probably really good at physical activities and learning through movement. You may need to **draw your finger over a diagram** to remember it, **"tap out" the steps** needed to solve a problem, or **"feel" yourself writing or typing** a formula.

SCHEDULING STUDY TIME

You should review your class notes regularly to ensure that you have a clear understanding of all the new material you learned. Reviewing your lessons on a regular basis helps you to learn and remember ideas and concepts. It also reduces the quantity of material that you need to study prior to a test. Establishing a study schedule will help you to make the best use of your time.

Regardless of the type of study schedule you use, you may want to consider the following suggestions to maximize your study time and effort:

- Organize your work so that you begin with the most challenging material first.
- Divide the subject's content into small, manageable chunks.
- Alternate regularly between your different subjects and types of study activities in order to maintain your interest and motivation.
- Make a daily list with headings like "Must Do," "Should Do," and "Could Do."
- Begin each study session by quickly reviewing what you studied the day before.
- Maintain your usual routine of eating, sleeping, and exercising to help you concentrate better for extended periods of time.

CREATING STUDY NOTES

MIND-MAPPING OR WEBBING

Use the key words, ideas, or concepts from your reading or class notes to create a *mind map* or *web* (a diagram or visual representation of the given information). A mind map or web is sometimes referred to as a knowledge map.

- Write the key word, concept, theory, or formula in the centre of your page.

- Write down related facts, ideas, events, and information and then link them to the central concept with lines.

- Use coloured markers, underlining, or other symbols to emphasize things such as relationships, time lines, and important information.

- The following examples of a Frayer Model illustrate how this technique can be used to study scientific vocabulary.

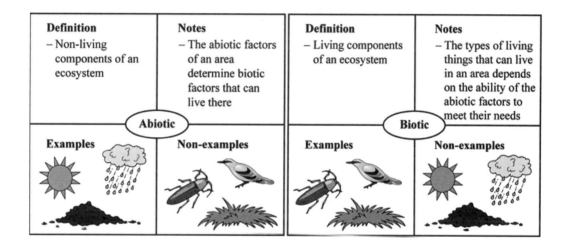

INDEX CARDS

To use index cards while studying, follow these steps:

- Write a key word or question on one side of an index card.

- On the reverse side, write the definition of the word, answer to the question, or any other important information that you want to remember.

What is the difference between heat and thermal energy?

What is the difference between heat and thermal energy?

Thermal energy is the total energy of the particles in a solid, liquid, or gas.
Heat is the amount of thermal energy transferred between objects.

SYMBOLS AND STICKY NOTES—IDENTIFYING IMPORTANT INFORMATION

Use symbols to mark your class notes. For example, an exclamation mark (!) might be used to point out something that must be learned well because it is a very important idea. A question mark (?) may highlight something that you are not certain about, and a diamond (◊) or asterisk (*) could highlight interesting information that you want to remember.

- Use sticky notes when you are not allowed to put marks in books.

- Use sticky notes to mark a page in a book that contains an important diagram, formula, explanation, etc.

- Use sticky notes to mark important facts in research books.

MEMORIZATION TECHNIQUES

- **Association** relates new learning to something you already know. For example, to remember the spelling difference between *dessert* and *desert*, recall that the word *sand* has only one *s*. So, because there is sand in a desert, the word *desert* only has on *s*.

- **Mnemonic** devices are sentences that you create to remember a list or group of items. For example, the first letter of each word in the phrase "**E**very **G**ood **B**oy **D**eserves **F**udge" helps you to remember the names of the lines on the treble clef staff (E, G, B, D, and F) in music.

- **Acronyms** are words that are formed from the first letters or parts of the words in a group. For example, **RADAR** is actually an acronym for **Ra**dio **D**etecting **A**nd **R**anging, and **MASH** is an acronym for **M**obile **A**rmy **S**urgical **H**ospital. **HOMES** helps you to remember the names of the five Great Lakes (**H**uron, **O**ntario, **M**ichigan, **E**rie, and **S**uperior).

- **Visualizing** requires you to use your mind's eye to "see" a chart, list, map, diagram, or sentence as it is in your textbook or notes, on the chalk board or computer screen, or in a display.

- **Initialisms** are abbreviations that are formed from the first letters or parts of the words in a group. Unlike acronyms, initialisms cannot be pronounced as a word themselves. For example, **BEDMAS** is an initialism for the order of operations in math (**B**rackets, **E**xponents, **D**ivide, **M**ultiply, **A**dd, **S**ubtract).

KEY STRATEGIES FOR REVIEWING

Reviewing textbook material, class notes, and handouts should be an ongoing activity. Spending time reviewing becomes more critical when you are preparing for tests. You may find some of the following review strategies useful when studying during your scheduled study time.

- Before reading a selection, preview it by noting the headings, charts, graphs, and chapter questions.
- Before reviewing a unit, note the headings, charts, graphs and chapter questions.
- Highlight key concepts, vocabulary, definitions and formulas.
- Skim the paragraph and note the key words, phrases, and information.
- Carefully read over each step in a procedure.
- Draw a picture or diagram to help make the concept clearer.

KEY STRATEGIES FOR SUCCESS: A CHECKLIST

Review, review, review: review is a huge part of doing well at school and preparing for tests. Here is a checklist for you to keep track of how many suggested strategies for success you are using. Read each question and then put a check mark (✓) in the correct column. Look at the questions where you have checked the "No" column. Think about how you might try using some of these strategies to help you do your best at school.

KEY Strategies for Success	Yes	No
Do you attend school regularly?		
Do you know your personal learning style—how you learn best?		
Do you spend 15 to 30 minutes a day reviewing your notes?		
Do you study in a quiet place at home?		
Do you clearly mark the most important ideas in your study notes?		
Do you use sticky notes to mark texts and research books?		
Do you practise answering multiple-choice and written-response questions?		
Do you ask your teacher for help when you need it?		
Are you maintaining a healthy diet and sleep routine?		
Are you participating in regular physical activity?		

BIOLOGICAL DIVERSITY

<table>
<tr><th colspan="4">Table of Correlations</th></tr>
<tr><th>Specific Expectation</th><th>Practice Questions</th><th>Unit Test Questions</th><th>2006 PAT</th></tr>
<tr><td colspan="4">Students will:</td></tr>
<tr><td colspan="4">A1. Investigate and interpret diversity among species and within species, and describe how diversity contributes to species survival.</td></tr>
<tr><td>A.1.1 observe variations in living things and describe examples of variation among species and within species</td><td>1, 2, 3</td><td>3</td><td></td></tr>
<tr><td>A.1.2 identify examples of niches, and describe the role of variation in enabling closely related living things to survive in the same ecosystem</td><td>4, 5, 6</td><td>1, 2</td><td>4, NR1</td></tr>
<tr><td>A.1.3 investigate and interpret dependencies among species that link the survival of one species to the survival of others
• identify examples of symbiotic relationships
• classify symbiotic relationships as mutualism, commensalism, parasitism</td><td>7, 8, 9</td><td>10</td><td></td></tr>
<tr><td>A.1.4 identify the role of variation in species survival under changing environmental conditions</td><td>10, 11</td><td>11</td><td></td></tr>
<tr><td colspan="4">A2. Investigate the nature of reproductive processes and their role in transmitting species characteristics.</td></tr>
<tr><td>A.2.1 distinguish between sexual and asexual reproduction, and identify and interpret examples of asexual and sexual reproduction in different species by:
• describing mechanisms of asexual reproduction including binary fission, budding and the production of spores
• describing mechanisms of sexual reproduction
• describing examples of organisms that show both sexual and asexual reproduction
• describing the formation of zygote and embryo in plant and animal reproduction</td><td>12, 13</td><td>NR1, 5</td><td>3</td></tr>
<tr><td>A.2.2 describe examples of variation of characteristics within a species, and identify examples of both discrete and continuous variation</td><td>14</td><td>4</td><td></td></tr>
<tr><td>A.2.3 investigate the transmission of characteristics from parents to offspring, and identify examples of characteristics in offspring that are:
• the same as the characteristics of both parents
• the same as the characteristics of one parent
• intermediate between parent characteristics
• different from both parents</td><td>15, 16</td><td></td><td></td></tr>
<tr><td>A.2.4 distinguish those characteristics that are heritable from those that are not heritable, and identify characteristics for which heredity and environment may both play a role</td><td>17, 18</td><td></td><td>10</td></tr>
</table>

A3.	Describe, in general terms, the role of genetic materials in the continuity and variation of species characteristics; and investigate and interpret related technologies.			
A.3.1 describe, in general terms, the relationship of chromosomes, genes and DNA	19, 20	7, 12, 13	
A.3.2 distinguish between cell division that leads to identical daughter cells, as in binary fission and mitosis, and cell division that leads to formation of sex cells, as in meiosis; and describe, in general terms, the synthesis of genetic materials that takes place during fertilization	21, 22, 23	8, 9	1
A.3.3 compare sexual and asexual reproduction, in terms of the advantages and disadvantages	24, 25	6, NR2	5
A.3.4 distinguish between, and identify examples of, natural and artificial selection	26, 27	WR1	6, 8
A.3.5 describe, in simple terms, some genetic technologies; and identify questions and issues related to their application	28		2
A4.	Identify impacts of human action on species survival and variation within species, and analyze related issues for personal and public decision making.			
A.4.1 describe the relative abundance of species on Earth and in different environments	29, 30, 31	14	
A.4.2 describe ongoing changes in biological diversity through extinction and extirpation of native species, and investigate the role of environmental factors in causing these changes	32, 33, 34	WR2, WR3	9, 21
A.4.3 evaluate the success and limitations of various local and global strategies for minimizing loss of species diversity	35		
A.4.4 investigate and describe the use of biotechnology in environmental, agricultural or forest management; and identify potential impacts and issues	36	15	

BIOLOGICAL DIVERSITY

A.1.1 *observe variations in living things and describe examples of variation among species and within species*

VARIATIONS OF SPECIES

A **species** can be defined as a group of organisms that is distinct from any other group of organisms. They share common characteristics and are capable of reproducing with each other to produce fertile offspring. Reproduction involving two individuals is called **sexual reproduction** and results in genetic variation.

Genetic variation is inherent in any natural population, and it arises due to spontaneous mutation and genetic recombination of an organism's DNA. Genetic variation translates into the observable variation that exists in the characteristics both within a given population of organisms and between populations of different organisms.

Natural selection promotes the adaptation of an organism to its environment by acting on these variations and selecting for the traits that better enable the organism to compete, survive, and reproduce. For example, during the Industrial Revolution, natural selection resulted in a shift toward the dark-coloured moth of the peppered moth population. This was because an increase in pollution in the environment provided dark-coloured moths with a camouflage advantage against predators. If the adaptations necessary for the organism to survive are fundamentally different from the original organism, a new species may develop. This is a process known as **speciation**.

Practice Questions: 1, 2, 3

A.1.2 *identify examples of niches, and describe the role of variation in enabling closely related living things to survive in the same ecosystem*

VARIATION AND NICHES

Members of a species that are living in the same area and sharing resources form a **population**. Populations of different species in an area form a **community**.

Within a community, animals occupy a specific niche. The term **niche** refers to an organism's habits and habitat within the community. It includes things like what the animal eats and what effect it has on the habitat and other species. The niches of a population of a species can vary depending on differences in the area it inhabits. This is due to differences in food supply and competitors in the area. Niches can also change throughout an individual organism's lifespan. A larval mosquito lives in an aquatic niche, but adult mosquitoes inhabit a terrestrial niche.

When two species occupy a common habitat, it is possible that they could compete for the same resources. This is referred to as **interspecies competition**, and it leads to a decrease in each species' share of the resources. This can lead to starvation and death. Thus, interspecies competition limits the size of populations in an area.

In order for similar species to coexist in the same area, they need to have slightly different niches. This means that they do not directly compete for resources; instead, they divide resources among them. This is called **resource partitioning**.

Practice Questions: 4, 5, 6

A.1.3   investigate and interpret dependencies among species that link the survival of one species to the survival of others

- *identify examples of symbiotic relationships*
- *classify symbiotic relationships as mutualism, commensalism, parasitism*

DEPENDENCIES AMONG SPECIES

Species of living things interact with each other. Each species depends on many other species in the environment. For example, plants use sunlight, carbon dioxide, water, and nutrients during photosynthesis to store energy and release oxygen. The oxygen produced by plants is used by animals for respiration. Plants also serve as food for herbivores.

Plants also provide shade and a habitat for many animals. In turn, the plants depend on insects for pollination. Carnivores depend on herbivores and omnivores as food sources. Decomposers break down dead and decaying plants and animals.

Interaction among different species is usually brief since it is mostly for the purpose of obtaining food. In some cases, however, interaction continues for a longer period of time. These are called **symbiotic associations**. In symbiosis, at least one member is benefited. The other may be

- relatively unaffected (commensalism)
- also benefited (mutualism)
- harmed (parasitism)

Commensalism is an association in which only one organism benefits, but the other is not harmed. For example, one organism may consume the unused food of another as in the case of the remora and the shark. When the shark feeds, the remora picks up the scraps. The shark does not prey on the remora. Another example of commensalism is the relationship between a robin and a tree. The robin picks up sticks and twigs that it finds on the ground and builds a nest up in the branches of the tree. The robin benefits by having shelter, and the tree is unaffected by the robin's presence.

Mutualism is an association in which both organisms benefit. For example, lichen is made up of both fungus and algae. The fungal cells in lichen benefit because the algal cells produce food for them through photosynthesis. The algal cells also benefit from this relationship because the fungus prevents their dehydration. Another example of mutualism is the roots of legume plants and nitrogen-fixing bacteria.

Parasitism is an association in which one organism benefits and the other organism is harmed. The organism that benefits is called the **parasite**, whereas the one that is harmed is the **host**. A parasite lives on or in the body of the host and obtains nourishment from it. For example, viruses, bacteria, fungi, protozoans, flatworms, nematodes, and some insects can be parasites on different plants and animals.

Practice Questions: 7, 8, 9

A.1.4   identify the role of variation in species survival under changing environmental conditions

VARIATION AND SPECIES SURVIVAL

As the environment changes, species exhibit some variations that are essential for their survival. Environmental changes do not only mean changes in climate, but also changes in availability of food, spread of new diseases, and the presence of predators. These all have an effect on the survival of the species. Variation within a population that allows the species to adapt to a new environment can lead to the survival of that species. For example, the banded snail lives in a variety of habitats: dark beaches, oak woods, or leafy green meadows. Its shell colour varies from yellow to pink to brown. It changes colour in the spring and summer to blend with its environment. Because of such variability, the snail can protect itself from predation and is better adapted to survive.

Practice Questions: 10, 11

A.2.1 distinguish between sexual and asexual reproduction, and identify and interpret examples of asexual and sexual reproduction in different species by:

- *describing mechanisms of asexual reproduction including binary fission, budding and the production of spores*
- *describing mechanisms of sexual reproduction*
- *describing examples of organisms that show both sexual and asexual reproduction*
- *describing the formation of zygote and embryo in plant and animal reproduction*

ASEXUAL REPRODUCTION

Asexual reproduction results in the production of offspring that are genetically identical to the parent. Asexual reproduction does not involve specific sex cells, but rather it involves all the body cells. It involves only one parent.
The offspring from asexual reproduction inherits identical characteristics to the single parent, so it is identical to its parent. Different forms of asexual reproduction are binary fission, budding, spore formation, and vegetative reproduction.

During **binary fission**, one cell splits into two cells, resulting in the production of two identical individuals. Bacteria and some protists reproduce through binary fission.

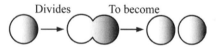

During **budding**, the parent produces a small bud, which detaches from the parent and develops into an identical individual. Budding takes place in yeast, hydra, and corals.

Some fungi and non-flowering plants, such as ferns, produce **spores**. Each spore develops into a new individual that is identical to the parent.

Vegetative reproduction is a form of reproduction that does not involve the formation of seeds. For example, cuttings of a coleus plant, runners in strawberries, tubers in potatoes, and bulbs in daffodils are various means by which vegetative reproduction can occur.

SEXUAL REPRODUCTION

Reproduction that involves two individuals is called **sexual reproduction**. Most species of animals and flowering plants undergo sexual reproduction. The offspring of sexual reproduction show characteristics of both parents.

SEXUAL REPRODUCTION IN ANIMALS

Sexual reproduction involves specialized cells known as **gametes**. Male gametes are called **sperm**, and the female gametes are known as **egg cells**. The union of a sperm cell and an egg cell occurs during **fertilization**. A **zygote** is formed as a result of fertilization. The zygote divides repeatedly to form an **embryo**. The development of an embryo may take place inside the female parent (as in mammals) or take place outside the body in an egg (as in birds and reptiles). The new individuals may resemble one parent more than the other but are not identical to either parent.

SEXUAL REPRODUCTION IN PLANTS

Plants that reproduce sexually produce flowers. Some flowers are large and showy, while others are small and inconspicuous. The flower contains **stamens**, which produce **pollen grains**.

Plant Reproductive Organs

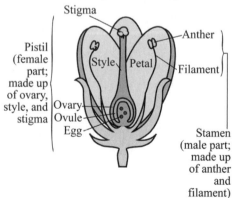

The male gametes are produced and contained in pollen grains. **Pistils**, which contain ovules, are responsible for producing the female gametes. During pollination, pollen grains from the **anther** are transferred to the **stigma** of the pistil.

The union of the male and female gametes takes place through fertilization. The resulting zygote divides to form an embryo. The embryo becomes the seed. When the conditions are favourable, the seeds germinate to produce new plants. A process called **cross-fertilization** occurs when the pollen of one plant is able to fertilize the female gametes of another plant. This often happens when the pollen is carried to another plant by wind or other animals.

SEXUAL AND ASEXUAL REPRODUCTION IN ONE ORGANISM

Some organisms are able to reproduce both sexually and asexually. In some species of grass, roses, and sunflowers, the embryo develops in the seed without a male gamete. In aphids, the female can produce other female aphids without fertilization. The young females are born instead of being hatched from eggs. Sponges also exhibit both types of reproduction.

Practice Questions: 12, 13

A.2.2   describe examples of variation of characteristics within a species, and identify examples of both discrete and continuous variation

DISCRETE VERSUS CONTINUOUS VARIATION

Discrete variation is the difference in characteristics that have a defined form. An organism either has a certain characteristic or it does not. For example, a person either has green eyes or he does not. Some people can roll their tongues, while others cannot. Some people have a free earlobe; others have an attached earlobe.

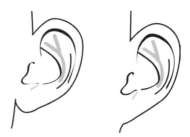

Continuous variation describes the range of a heritable characteristic. Height is a good example of this. The normal human height range is well over one metre, with the petite at one end, the very tall at the other, and most people falling somewhere in between.

Practice Question: 14

A.2.3   investigate the transmission of characteristics from parents to offspring, and identify examples of characteristics in offspring that are:

- *the same as the characteristics of both parents*
- *the same as the characteristics of one parent*
- *intermediate between parent characteristics*
- *different from both parents*

A.2.5   identify examples of dominant and recessive characteristics and recognize that dominance and recessiveness provide only a partial explanation for the variation of characteristics in offspring

TRANSMISSION OF CHARACTERISTICS

The transmission of characteristics from parents to offspring takes place through **genes**. Genes have several possible forms. These forms are called **alleles**. This process of transmission is called **inheritance**.

An individual produced by crossing two purebred parents that differ in a trait is known as a **hybrid**. After crossbreeding, the trait that is able to express itself is called the **dominant trait**, and the one that does not express itself is called the **recessive trait**.

In this picture, the colour purple is the dominant trait and white is the recessive trait because all four offspring flowers are purple.

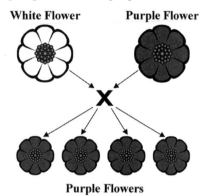

White Flower   **Purple Flower**

X

Purple Flowers

Sometimes, the dominant and recessive traits are blended together. For example, when a purebred red-flowered snapdragon plant is crossed with a purebred white-flowered plant, the offspring have neither red nor white flowers, but pink flowers. This pattern of inheritance is called **incomplete dominance**. Both the red-flower allele and the white-flower allele played a role in determining the flower colour of the offspring.

The inheritance of characteristics can be summarized as follows:

- If the offspring have the same characteristics as both parents, it is a result of pure breeding.

- If the offspring have the same characteristics as one of the parents, it is a result of crossbreeding and a dominant-recessive pattern of inheritance.

- If the offspring have intermediate characteristics of both parents, it is a result of crossbreeding and incomplete dominance.

- If the offspring differ from both parents, it is a result of a combination of several possible alleles for each trait.

Practice Questions: 15, 16

A.2.4   distinguish those characteristics that are heritable from those that are not heritable, and identify characteristics for which heredity and environment may both play a role

HERITABLE AND NON-HERITABLE CHARACTERISTICS

Characteristics of parents are transmitted to the next generation by the process of **heredity**. Some characteristics are inherited, while other characteristics are not. **Heritable** characteristics are passed on from one generation to another. An example of this is skin colour. **Non-heritable** characteristics, however, are acquired. They are not transferred by genes to the next generation. A father who is a very good soccer player would have to teach his children how to play the game. The children would have to learn, or acquire, the skills of playing soccer.

Sometimes, variations in individuals are a result of environmental factors. If two identical twins are separated and live in areas with different climatic conditions, they may develop some variation in their skin colour. The twin who lives in a warmer climate may have darker skin. Variations caused by interactions with the environment are not heritable, rather they are acquired.

Practice Questions: 17, 18

A.3.1   describe, in general terms, the relationship of chromosomes, genes and DNA

CHROMOSOMES, GENES, AND DNA

Deoxyribonucleic acid (DNA) is found in the nucleus of cells. Watson and Crick revealed the structure of DNA and explained that it is the chemical building block that carries a wide range of instructions responsible for the diversity of traits.

DNA is a spiral-shaped, double-helix molecule made of **nucleotides**. Each nucleotide contains deoxyribose sugar, phosphate, and four types of nitrogen bases called guanine, cytosine, adenine, and thiamine. The arrangement of these bases forms a code that cells can be read. Millions of combinations are possible.

Chromosomes are packages of DNA. In plant and animal cells, the chromosomes are present inside the nucleus. Every organism has a specific number of chromosomes, and they usually come in pairs. Each human cell contains 46 chromosomes. All the cells of the human body, except the gametes, have a complete set of 23 pairs of chromosomes. Dogs have 78 chromosomes in each cell. Cats have 38 chromosomes in each cell.

The 23 chromosomes of a male human

Genes are the portions of an organism's DNA that carry genetic information and are responsible for the inheritance of an organism's traits. Genes and the traits that they produce are passed from the parent to the offspring.

Genes are located on chromosomes. Like chromosomes, genes also exist in pairs called alleles. **Alleles** are responsible for expressing variations or characteristics. Alleles that are dominant are able to express themselves. Alleles that are recessive are unable to express themselves, and the characteristic trait does not appear.

Practice Questions: 19, 20

A.3.2 distinguish between cell division that leads to identical daughter cells, as in binary fission and mitosis, and cell division that leads to formation of sex cells, as in meiosis; and describe, in general terms, the synthesis of genetic materials that takes place during fertilization

CELL DIVISION

The multiplication of the somatic (body) cells takes place by cell division called **mitosis**. Mitosis begins with a cell duplicating all its contents (including the chromosomes). Then, half the contents are pulled to each side of the cell. Mitosis is complete when a membrane forms in the middle and results in the production of two new cells with the same number of chromosomes. Mitosis is responsible for growth and repair in multicellular organisms.

Meiosis is the type of cell division that takes place in the formation of gametes (egg and sperm). Just as with mitosis, the cell duplicates its chromosomes. However, in meiosis, the cell divides twice. This results in cells (gametes) that have half the chromosome number of the original cell.

Normal Meiosis

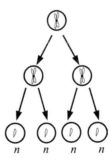

When a male sperm cell and female egg cell unite to form a zygote, the chromosome number is restored.

Practice Questions: 21, 22, 23

A.3.3   compare sexual and asexual reproduction, in terms of the advantages and disadvantages

COMPARING ASEXUAL AND SEXUAL REPRODUCTION

Asexual reproduction results in the formation of a large number of cells very quickly. A single bacterial cell can reproduce asexually every 20 minutes. At this rate of division, it is possible to have over 1 million bacteria produced in a seven-hour period. This is an advantage of asexual reproduction: in a short span of time, innumerable new cells are produced. However, asexual reproduction can be disadvantageous. Entire populations of a species may be destroyed if the conditions are not suitable for survival. For example, millions of bacteria can be destroyed by administering antibiotics.

Sexual reproduction involves two parents. The offspring receive characteristics from each parent. A lot of variation can exist as a result of the recombination of genes, and these variations are useful for survival during unfavourable conditions. The major disadvantage of sexual reproduction is that it takes a lot of time and consumes a lot of energy. When humans reproduce, the fertilization process must occur, and then the embryo needs nine months to grow and develop inside the mother. The amount of time and energy this takes limits the number of offspring that are produced.

Practice Questions: 24, 25

A.3.4   distinguish between, and identify examples of, natural and artificial selection

NATURAL AND ARTIFICIAL SELECTION

If a species lives in a changing environment, the individuals often exhibit a great deal of variation among themselves in order to adapt to the changes. Survival of a species is affected by certain changes like the spread of disease, the presence of predators, or the scarcity of food resources. The species that exhibits some variation will be more likely to adapt to the new environment and will have a better chance of surviving.

Natural selection is a process in which the environment helps the species to survive. It is a process in nature that results in the fittest organisms producing offspring. The species that is able to adapt by showing variability in traits becomes the fittest. Nature selects this individual to produce new offspring. Other individuals either perish or migrate. The Galápagos Island finches represent one of the most well-known examples of natural selection. There is an extremely diverse range of 13 different finch species on the island. The primary difference observed among the different finch species is variation in their beak shape. Each species has a beak shape that is uniquely adapted to the particular food resource it eats. After studying the finch population on the island, Charles Darwin concluded that the beak structure changed over time by natural selection as each finch species adapted to its environment.

The Galápagos Island finches

Artificial selection is the process in which the individuals with the most suitable traits are selected artificially (by humans not by nature) and are allowed to produce offspring. For example, certain cows produce only small amounts of milk, whereas others produce large amounts of milk. A farmer who wants cows that produce a lot of milk would only allow those cows that produce large amounts of milk to breed. The result is offspring that are good milk producers.

In artificial selection, the intervention of humans ensures that only individuals with more desirable traits produce offspring.

Practice Questions: 26, 27

A.3.5 *describe, in simple terms, some genetic technologies; and identify questions and issues related to their application*

A.4.4 *investigate and describe the use of biotechnology in environmental, agricultural or forest management; and identify potential impacts and issues*

GENETIC TECHNOLOGIES

Artificial selection in plants and animals has led to some new technologies. Some of these technologies include cloning, artificial reproductive technology, and genetic engineering.

A **clone** is an exact copy of something. It can be a copy of a single gene, a cell, or an entire organism. Scientists often create plant clones. To do this, the cells from a plant with a particular trait are removed and are placed in the nutrients and hormones required by those cells for growth. These cells will develop into seedlings and are transplanted in soil. New plants develop in a short span of time.

Artificial reproductive technology refers to artificial methods of fusing male and female gametes. In artificial insemination, the sperm of a male animal with a desired trait are inserted into many female animals of the same species. The females give birth to offspring with the desirable traits. The advantage of this is that the desirable traits from the male are passed down to many offspring.

Genetic engineering is the technology of altering the DNA of an organism. For example, bacteria can be genetically engineered to produce life-saving insulin to control diabetes. Through genetic engineering, pest-resistant crops can be created, thereby reducing the use of pesticides. This could be beneficial to the environment by preventing the excessive use of pesticides.

Development of these technologies allows desirable traits to be passed on to future generations of offspring. However, these technologies reduce genetic variation. This makes the population more susceptible to being wiped out by a disease or changes in the environment.

Practice Questions: 28, 36

A.4.1 *describe the relative abundance of species on Earth and in different environments*

DISTRIBUTION OF LIFE ON EARTH

The existence of life on Earth is made possible because of water and the presence of an atmosphere containing oxygen. Biologists have identified around 1.5 million species of plants and animals.

The species on Earth are not evenly distributed. Tropical rain forests in equatorial regions have the greatest biological diversity. The Arctic and Antarctic regions contain the least biological diversity. This is because these environments have very cold temperatures and little food. This makes the region inhospitable to many plants and animals.

Practice Questions: 29, 30, 31

A.4.2 *describe ongoing changes in biological diversity through extinction and extirpation of native species, and investigate the role of environmental factors in causing these changes*

EXTIRPATION AND EXTINCTION

Biological diversity is gradually decreasing as a result of urbanization, industrialization, agriculture, and forestry. In fact, certain species of plants and animals are disappearing from the planet completely. This poses a threat to these living resources.

When an animal or plant species becomes so rare that it is threatened with extinction, it is called an **endangered species**. Some species that were once quite common have been hunted until few remain. Harsh environmental conditions, epidemic diseases, or other natural disasters can lead to the extinction or extirpation of endangered species. An example of an endangered species is the whooping crane. The whooping crane population has been affected by habitat loss.

Extinction means the disappearance of every individual of a species from the entire planet. Often, extinction of a species occurs over a long period of time. Catastrophic events, such as climate change, earthquakes, floods, or volcanic eruptions, are likely to have been the cause of mass extinctions. Scientists believe that it may have been an extreme climate change that resulted in the disappearance of the dinosaur.

Extirpation means local extinction, that is, the disappearance of a species from a particular area. While that species is not found in that region, there are still populations of the species elsewhere on the planet. The swift fox had been extirpated from the grasslands of southern Alberta. It is only through conservation practices that the swift fox population is now recovering.

NATURAL CAUSES OF EXTINCTION AND EXTIRPATION

There are some natural causes of extinction and extirpation. Variation within species is important, but natural selection is a very slow process. A harsh change to the environment may be too quick for a species to develop variations and adapt. Changes that result from floods, volcanic eruptions, and earthquakes can cause species extirpation.

HUMAN CAUSES OF EXTINCTION

Human activities have a great impact on biological diversity. Urbanization, overhunting, construction of dams, roads, and buildings, agricultural development, pollution, and excessive use of pesticides, herbicides, and fertilizers can cause a decrease in biological diversity. Humans have also put certain animals and plants in danger of becoming endangered or extinct by introducing non-native species that compete for resources with species already in the ecosystem.

EFFECTS OF EXTINCTION AND EXTIRPATIONS

Extinction and extirpation of a species have a tremendous effect on the biological diversity in an area. When a species disappears from an area or from Earth, many other species are affected. For example, when one species becomes extinct, other animals that have relied upon it as a food source decrease in numbers. These animals must find another available food source or risk becoming endangered or extinct themselves.

Practice Questions: 32, 33, 34

A.4.3   evaluate the success and limitations of various local and global strategies for minimizing loss of species diversity

PRESERVING BIOLOGICAL DIVERSITY

Biological diversity should be preserved worldwide, and various groups are taking action. The focus is on promoting the sustainable use of resources and managing human activity.

These are some of the steps the Canadian government has taken to conserve biological diversity:

- Developed protected areas like national parks such as Banff and Jasper.

- Monitors and controls the spread of non-native, invasive species

- Implemented restoration programs that aim to protect endangered species and restore their damaged habitats.

- Created policies and laws on the hunting of endangered species.

- Set up seed banks to preserve genetic material in case of a catastrophe.

Practice Question: 35

PRACTICE QUESTIONS—BIOLOGICAL DIVERSITY

1. Which of the following statements about variations within species is **false**?
    A. Variations help species adapt to changing environments.
    B. Variations better equip species for survival.
    C. Variations produce new traits in species.
    D. Variations make species static.

Use the following information to answer the next question.

Variation in a species is an important factor that leads to evolution.

2. Variations within a species are not caused by
    A. fertilization
    B. mutation
    C. meiosis
    D. cloning

3. Variations within species are the result of
    A. growth
    B. nutrition
    C. metabolism
    D. sexual reproduction

4. The term niche describes
    A. a group of the same organisms in the same area
    B. the role an organism plays in an ecosystem
    C. where an organism lives
    D. what an organism eats

5. Several species of finches, each with a different beak shape, were discovered on the Galápagos Islands. The **best** explanation of why these finches evolved a variety of beak shapes is that they adapted to
    A. obtain different types of food
    B. defend against different enemies
    C. gather different nesting materials
    D. perform different courtship rituals

Use the following information to answer the next question.

When similar species coexist in an area, they have slightly different niches. They do not compete for resources; instead they divide the resources among them.

6. The type of arrangement described is called
    A. specialization
    B. natural selection
    C. artificial selection
    D. resource partitioning

7. Commensalism, parasitism, and mutualism are examples of a dependence relationship called
    A. niches
    B. predation
    C. symbiosis
    D. extirpation

Use the following information to answer the next question.

The suckerfish, *Echeneis*, has a dorsal fin modified to form a sucker-like organ, which helps it attach to the underside of a shark. This interaction provides protection to the suckerfish, but it does not harm the shark.

8. What type of dependency does the given interaction suggest?

A. Parasitic

B. Mutualistic

C. Cooperative

D. Commensal

Use the following information to answer the next question.

Organism X lives in the body of organism Y. X feeds on nutrients from the body of Y without providing any benefit to Y. The nutrients that X takes from Y are needed by Y in order to survive.

9. This situation describes a relationship that is

A. parasitic

B. mutualistic

C. cooperative

D. commensal

Use the following information to answer the next question.

Three Closely Related Species of Foxes

Arctic Fox   Deciduous   Desert Fox
        Forest Fox

Fox species have evolved different ear shape and size to adapt to their environment. These successful characteristics were passed down to the next generation to ensure survival.

10. The **most likely** reason a desert fox has larger ears than the other two species of foxes is to ensure that it can

A. regulate its body heat and temperature

B. detect impending danger

C. locate its potential prey

D. find running water

Use the following information to answer the next question.

These are some characteristics of different organisms:

I. *Hydrangea* bears blue flowers in acidic soil and pinkish flowers in alkaline soil.

II. Plants growing in hot areas show greater growth of root systems.

III. Birds of a same species have slightly different calls.

IV. Adult human beings differ in height.

11. All phenomena listed are examples of

A. selection

B. mutation

C. variation

D. competition

Use the following information to answer the next question.

An adult hydra develops a swelling on the side of its body. Eventually, this swelling grows tentacles and starts to feed. The swelling breaks away from the mother hydra and floats freely until it lands on a surface where it attaches for support and starts to live independently.

12. Reproduction of this type is known **most specifically** as

    A. budding

    B. binary fission

    C. sexual reproduction

    D. asexual reproduction

13. The union of a male sperm cell with a female egg cell is referred to as

    A. pollination

    B. fertilization

    C. parthenogenesis

    D. asexual reproduction

Use the following information to answer the next question.

The giraffe has adapted with a long neck in order to eat foliage from tall trees. Certain giraffes, however, have longer necks and can reach the higher foliage.

14. The difference in neck length among giraffes is referred to as

    A. diversification

    B. discrete variation

    C. artificial selection

    D. continuous variation

15. An offspring having the same traits as both of its parents is a result of

    A. crossbreeding

    B. pure breeding

    C. artificial breeding

    D. random breeding

16. A red flower and a white flower are crossed. If the offspring has all red flowers, then it can be concluded that:

    A. red is a recessive trait and white is dominant

    B. red is a dominant trait and white is recessive

    C. red and white are both dominant traits

    D. red and white are both recessive traits

Use the following information to answer the next question.

It is commonly observed that blue-eyed parents produce offspring with blue eyes.

17. It can be concluded that eye colour is a

    A. heritable characteristic

    B. dominant characteristic

    C. recessive characteristic

    D. non-heritable characteristic

Use the following information to answer the next question.

Wolfgang plays the piano very well, but his son Charles does not.

18. The explanation for Charles's inability to play the piano is that playing piano is a

    A. heritable characteristic

    B. recessive characteristic

    C. dominant characteristic

    D. non-heritable characteristic

Use the following information to answer the next question.

The chromosome theory of heredity states that genes on chromosomes are responsible for the inherited characteristics of organisms.

19. Which of the following statements summarizes the given information?

    A. Genes exist in pairs.

    B. The human cell contains 46 chromosomes.

    C. Chromosomes are composed of DNA and protein.

    D. Genes determine hereditary traits.

20. Which of the following statements does **not** describe a major function of genetic material?

    A. It replicates itself.

    B. It stores information.

    C. It transfers information.

    D. It catalyzes chemical reactions.

21. Which of the following statements about cell division is **not** correct?

    A. Mitotic division produces eight cells at one time.

    B. Mitosis takes place in somatic body cells.

    C. The process of meiosis occurs only in sex cells.

    D. The process of meiosis produces a total of four cells, during two divisions.

22. Which of the following functions is **not** achieved through meiosis?

    A. Sexual reproduction

    B. Production of gametes

    C. Growth and cellular repair

    D. Recombination of genetic material

23. Mitosis is a type of cell division that is responsible for all of the following functions **except**

    A. reducing the number of chromosomes by half

    B. maintaining the number of chromosomes

    C. helping in growth and cellular repair

    D. increasing the size of the organism

Use the following information to answer the next question.

The jellyfish alternates between sexual and asexual reproduction.

24. An advantage of the jellyfish reproducing sexually is that sexual reproduction

    A. produces identical offspring

    B. allows for less crossing over of genetic material

    C. requires less energy to complete

    D. provides genetic variation in the offspring

25. In terms of energy consumption and the number of offspring that can be produced, asexual reproduction generally requires

    A. a lot of energy and produces a lot of offspring

    B. a lot of energy and produces a few offspring

    C. little energy and produces a lot of offspring

    D. little energy and produces a few offspring

Use the following information to answer the next question.

In southern England during the early 1800s, the mottled, light grey pepper moth was very common. During the day, it roosted on tree bark that was also light grey. As a result, the pepper moth was well camouflaged. Occasionally, a dark grey pepper moth was seen. By the mid-1800s, the Industrial Revolution was responsible for a lot of air pollution from coal-burning factories. Everything became covered in black soot, including the trunks of trees.

26. During the Industrial Revolution, natural selection affected the pepper moth population in that
    A. lighter colouring became more common in the population
    B. darker colouring became more common in the population
    C. different predators consumed the pepper moths
    D. the population became extinct

Use the following information to answer the next question.

At the end of the 1800s, the average sheep in Britain produced far more wool than did the average sheep at the beginning of the 1800s. This was most likely due to farmers choosing only the woolliest sheep as breeding stock.

27. The scenario is an example of
    A. artificial selection
    B. natural selection
    C. evolution
    D. cloning

Use the following information to answer the next question.

The beef industry in Alberta depends on artificial reproductive technologies to produce cattle with high-quality meat.

28. Alberta farmers are raising high-quality cattle by using modern reproductive technologies such as
    A. cloning
    B. natural selection
    C. genetic engineering
    D. artificial insemination

29. Compared to temperate regions, equatorial regions have
    A. a larger number and variety of species
    B. a smaller number and variety of species
    C. fewer species with more variety
    D. roughly the same number and variety of species, but with different characteristics from those in temperate regions

30. Which of the following categories has the highest species diversity on the planet?
    A. Birds
    B. Plants
    C. Insects
    D. Mammals

31. How many species of organisms are currently known to scientists?
    A. 1 to 2 thousand
    B. 1 to 2 million
    C. 1 to 2 billion
    D. 1 to 2 trillion

Use the following information to answer the next question.

In the late 1400s, spice traders first discovered dodo birds on the island of Mauritius, in the Indian Ocean. Ships were soon making regular stops to kill the large flightless birds for food. The slaughter of dodos continued until 1681, when dodos became extinct. Mauritius is also home to Calvaria trees. All Calvaria trees are more than 300 years old—none have begun to grow since the last dodo was killed. Calvaria nuts have been found in fossilized remains of dodo birds.

32. A reasonable hypothesis to explain why no new Calvaria trees began growing is that

A. dodos are required to pollinate the Calvaria flowers

B. spice traders used Calvaria wood for building and fires

C. pollution made it impossible for young Calvaria trees to grow

D. the Calvaria nut had to pass through the digestive system of a dodo before it could begin to grow

Use the following information to answer the next question.

Grizzly bears used to occupy areas from the Rocky Mountains to Manitoba. Human activities have had an impact on the range of grizzly bears. It is now only found along the Rocky Mountain Range.

33. A species like the grizzly bear is best described as

A. a biological species

B. an impacted species

C. an extirpated species

D. a bioindicator species

34. Which of the following reasons **cannot** be given as a cause of the decrease in worldwide biodiversity?

A. A greater dependence on wood for fuel

B. An increase in the demand for consumer goods

C. An increased need to clear land for agriculture

D. A decrease in human population growth in developing countries

35. Canada has designated many areas as national parks. According to a wildlife conservationist, the **best** reason to develop national parks is

A. to save the natural biodiversity of the area by maintaining the interactions that naturally occur there

B. to maintain a pristine region of land to be admired by all citizens now and into the future

C. to bolster local and provincial economies by providing a setting ideal for tourism

D. to stop the over-hunting of animals from legal and illegal hunting

36. Big, healthy corn cobs were developed by early aboriginal people through the use of

A. cloning

B. random chance

C. mutating genes

D. artificial selection

ANSWERS AND SOLUTIONS—PRACTICE QUESTIONS

1. D	10. A	19. D	28. D
2. D	11. C	20. D	29. A
3. D	12. A	21. A	30. C
4. B	13. B	22. C	31. B
5. A	14. D	23. A	32. D
6. D	15. B	24. D	33. C
7. C	16. B	25. C	34. D
8. D	17. A	26. B	35. A
9. A	18. D	27. A	36. D

1. D

Because of variations, species do not remain static. Rather, a species slowly modifies, contributing to the formation of a new species over time.

2. D

Cloning leads to the formation of organisms that have exactly the same genes as those of their parents. Therefore, cloning does not cause variations within species.

Fertilization, mutation, and meiosis all cause variations within species.

3. D

Differences in traits or variations within a species occur as a result of the interaction of genes before and during sexual reproduction, not because of metabolism, nutrition, or growth. Metabolism and growth are both examples of variations, not causes, and nutrition is external to a species.

4. B

A habitat is the locality where an organism lives. A niche is the role the organism plays in its habitat. Both the coyote and the owl live on the grassland region and eat mice and shrews. Therefore, they occupy the same habitat and niche.

5. A

Galapagos finches evolved variations in beak shape. This variation allows the finches to eat different types of foods. Having different food needs means less competition for food. This increases the chances of all species of finches surviving.

6. D

When similar species coexist in an area, they have slightly different niches; therefore, they do not compete with each other. This is called resource partitioning. One species of bird may live in the top half of a tree. Another similar species may live in the bottom half of the tree.

7. C

Commensalism, parasitism, and mutualism are all examples of symbiosis. Symbiosis is an interaction between species that benefits at least one of the participating species.

8. D

The suckerfish benefits from attaching itself to the shark, but the shark is not harmed. This dependence is called commensalism.

9. A

A parasitic relationship is an association between organisms where one member lives off the other member.

10. A

The most likely reason for the difference in ear size between members of the fox species is that there is a need to adapt to climate. Since deserts are warmer than the other locations, the fox would need large ears to keep cool.

11. C

Variation refers to the differences observed among individuals of the same species and the offspring of the same parents. Variations make some individuals fitter in the struggle for survival. They help individuals adapt to changes in the environment.

12. A

Budding is a type of asexual reproduction used by some multicellular organisms.

13. B

The union of a male and female gamete is called fertilization. It is an important process in sexual reproduction. The fusion of gametes results in the formation of a zygote.

14. D

Variations among individuals in a species can be discrete or continuous. The giraffe's neck length is an example of a continuous variation. In a continuous variation a series of differences in a characteristic may occur. For example, giraffes can vary in height and weight.

Discrete variations are "either-or" variations. Either the hair colour is blond or it is black.

15. B

When the offspring resembles both the parents, it is a result of pure breeding. Purebred refers to a plant or animal that has ancestors all with the same form of traits. When two individuals with different traits are crossed, they are said to be crossbred and the offspring is called a hybrid. Cross breading is a type of random breeding.

16. B

When two plants with red and white flowers are crossed and all the offspring have red flowers, it is because red is dominant and is able to be expressed in the next generation. White is recessive because it fails to be expressed in the second generation.

17. A

Blue-eyed parents produce blue-eyed offspring. Characteristics such as eye colour that pass from one generation to the next are called heritable characteristics. Dominant and recessive characteristics are those that express or do not express themselves in the next generation. Non-heritable characteristics are not pass to the next generation.

18. D

The ability to play the piano is a non-heritable characteristic. The skill of playing piano is an acquired characteristic, and is not pass directly from the parents to the offspring.

19. D

The chromosome theory of heredity states that genes located on chromosomes determine hereditary traits. The traits are passed from parents to offspring through genes.

20. D

Catalyzing chemical reactions is not a major function of genetic material. Genetic material, however, can replicate and contains information that it stores and transmits from the parents to the offspring.

21. A

During the process of mitosis, only two cells are produced. During meiosis, four cells are produced. Mitosis takes place in somatic cells, whereas meiosis occurs in sex cells.

22. C

Growth and cellular repair is not achieved through meiosis. This is the function of mitosis. Meiotic division produces gametes.

23. A

Mitosis is not responsible for reducing the number of chromosomes to half. In meiotic division, the chromosomal number is reduced to half. Mitosis is a type of cell division that maintains the number of chromosomes in the next generation and helps in growth and cellular repair.

24. D

An advantage of sexual reproduction over asexual reproduction is that sexual reproduction provides genetic variation in the offspring. During sexual reproduction, gametes are formed by meiotic cell division. During meiosis, the exchange of genetic material takes place through crossing over, which provides genetic variation in the offspring.

25. C

Compared to sexual reproduction, asexual reproduction requires very little energy investment and is capable of producing large numbers of offspring. Gametes are not produced, and there is often no parental involvement or care for the offspring.

26. B

During the Industrial Revolution, as soot from factories darkened tree trunks, the darker-coloured moth became more common than the lighter-coloured moth. The darker-coloured moth camouflaged with the trunk and was better adapted for survival.

27. A

Artificial selection involves selective breeding by farmers or scientists to produce animals with certain desirable characteristics. Farmers interbred animals with the thickest wool.

28. D

High-quality cattle are produced by using modern reproductive technologies such as artificial insemination. The semen of a prize bull is collected and inserted in the womb of many cows. The calves produced will show the traits of the best bull.

29. A

Equatorial regions have the largest number and variety of species. These regions have the greatest number of plant species because conditions are favourable for their growth. The diverse plant species provide food and shelter to a wide variety of organisms.

30. C

Insects are the most abundant on Earth because they can survive in a variety of habitats. Also, they can adapt to a variety of climatic conditions.

31. B

Currently, around 1.5 million species of organisms are known to scientists.

32. D

It has been hypothesized that there must be something in the fluid of a dodo's digestive system that stimulates a Calvaria seed to start to grow. The Calvaria nut must have to be eaten by a dodo before it can germinate

33. C

The grizzly bear is called an extirpated species. Extirpation means local extinction, or disappearance of a species from a particular area. Because of habitat loss, the range of the grizzly bear has been reduced. They are now found only in the Rocky Mountains.

34. D

Biodiversity is reduced by human activities. Habitat loss due to human impact is the major cause of a reduction in biodiversity.

35. A

Designing a national park is an example of *in situ* conservation. The species remain in their natural habitat. All the interactions in the ecosystems are natural. Without the establishment of national parks and rules governing how much commercial development is allowed in parks, these areas would be subject to development according to supply and demand and would most likely become highly developed tourist destinations. Species would find it very difficult to survive in a habitat disturbed by humans.

36. D

Big, healthy corn cobs were developed by early aboriginal people using artificial selection. Corn was bred from the species of grass called teosinte. Seeds were gathered from the biggest and the healthiest corn plants and developed into new plants with these desirable traits. By using these seeds, they developed a more productive strain of corn plant.

UNIT TEST—BIOLOGICAL DIVERSITY

*Use the following information to answer
the next three questions.*

> While hiking through a meadow, Kerry spotted
> a small pond filled with activity.

1. The frogs and the mallard ducks that Kerry
   saw in the pond feed on small aquatic insects.
   This type of predator-prey food relationship
   is called

   A. mutualism

   B. parasitism

   C. competition

   D. resource partitioning

2. The pond is an interaction of living and
   non-living things. The term that describes a
   typical meadow pond is

   A. niche

   B. population

   C. ecosystem

   D. community

3. Which of the following statements about
   variations within species is **false**?

   A. Variations help species adapt to changing
   environments.

   B. Variations better equip species for
   survival.

   C. Variations produce new traits in species.

   D. Variations make species static.

*Use the following information to answer
the next question.*

> Julie collected data on the structure of the
> human ear from four members of her class.
>
>
>
> | Name | Type of Lobe |
> |------|--------------|
> | Jen | Attached lobe |
> | Matt | Free lobe |
> | Mia | Attached lobe |
> | Thai | Free lobe |

4. Which of the following two terms describe
   lobe traits?

   A. Heritable characteristic and
   continuous variation

   B. Heritable characteristic and
   discrete variation

   C. Non-heritable characteristic and
   discrete variation

   D. Non-heritable characteristic and
   continuous variation

Use the following information to answer the next question.

A male sperm unites with a female egg to produce a new individual. Some of the terms that describe this process are listed.

1. Fertilization   2. Gametes
3. Embryo   4. Zygote

Numerical Response

1. The order in which the numbered stages of development occur is ____, ____, ____, and ____. (Record your answer as a **four-digit** number.)

5. Which flower structure produces the male gamete?

A. Ovary

B. Stigma

C. Anther

D. Ovule

Use the following information to answer the next question.

Despite belonging to a single species, humans show great diversity in terms of the biological and physiological expression of their genetic makeup. This type of variation within a species is seen in many animals but is absent in organisms such as amoebas.

6. The absence of variation within a species of amoeba is a result of the fact that amoebas

A. are prokaryotic cells

B. do not photosynthesize

C. are unicellular in nature

D. do not reproduce sexually

Use the following information to answer the next question.

The following descriptors are about reproduction:

W. Results in variations in species

X. Requires specialized reproductive cells

Y. Requires a large amount of energy

Z. Results in individuals that are genetically identical

Numerical Response

2. Write the number 1 in the blank if the letter refers to sexual reproduction and the number 2 if the letter refers to asexual reproduction.

‾‾ ‾‾ ‾‾ ‾‾
 W   X   Y   Z
(Record your answer as a **four-digit** number.)

7. DNA is an important structural component of

A. the cell wall

B. a chloroplast

C. the cytoplasm

D. a chromosome

8. The division of human sex cells is referred to as

A. meiosis, which produces 23 chromosomes

B. mitosis, which produces 23 chromosomes

C. meiosis, which produces 46 chromosomes

D. mitosis, which produces 46 chromosomes

9. Which of the following situations is **not** an example of asexual reproduction?

A. A hydra producing a bud

B. A plant propagating from a root

C. Bacteria dividing by binary fission

D. An embryo developing from a zygote

Use the following information to answer the next question.

As a bee pollinates clusia flowers, it becomes covered with a sticky resin that contains a powerful antibiotic. This antibiotic kills bacteria in the bee hive.

10. The association of a bee and a clusia flower is an example of

A. parasitism

B. mutualism

C. commensalism

D. heterotrophism

11. Which of the following factors is important for the ensured survival of a species in a changing environment?

A. Symbiotic associations

B. Interspecies competition

C. Variation within a species

D. Ability to reproduce asexually

Use the following information to answer the next question.

If the structure of DNA is compared to a spiralling ladder, then each step would be made of paired molecules.

12. In this comparison, the steps of the DNA ladder are composed of

A. phosphates

B. nitrogen bases

C. sugars and phosphates

D. sugars and nitrogen bases

13. DNA does **not** contain

A. nucleotides

B. cytosine

C. guanine

D. uracil

14. Which of the following biomes has the **most diverse** life forms?

A. Deciduous forest

B. Rain forest

C. Grassland

D. Taiga

15. The **main** drawback in using hybridized species of plants or animals is that

A. the cost of producing them is too high

B. they usually fail to grow or live

C. genetic diversity is decreased

D. they are unable to reproduce

Written Response

1. What is the difference between artificial selection and natural selection?

(2 marks)

2. Describe the difference between an endangered species and an extinct species, and give an example of each.

(2 marks)

3. Indicate two human factors that have contributed to the loss of biodiversity in the prairie area of Alberta.

(2 marks)

ANSWERS AND SOLUTIONS—UNIT TEST

1. C	5. C	9. D	14. B
2. D	6. D	10. B	15. C
3. D	NR2. 1112	11. C	WR1. See Solution
4. B	7. D	12. B	WR2. See Solution
NR1. 2143	8. A	13. D	WR3. See Solution

1. C

The frogs and the mallard duck are in competition for the same food. Mutualism is a relationship where two species benefit from each other. In parasitism, one species benefits while the other is harmed. Resource partitioning refers to selecting a niche that does not interfere with the other species.

2. D

Since the pond represents a limited area, it is a community. A population refers to only one type of species (frogs) in a particular area. A niche deals more with the role that an organism has in an ecosystem. An ecosystem is made up of several communities.

3. D

Mutations are permanent changes in DNA or genes. Ultraviolet rays, nuclear materials, and certain chemicals can cause these mutations. Mutations can also be caused by improper copying of genetic information during cell division. Sexual reproduction results in genetic variations through the exchange and interaction of genetic material, not through mutations.

Sexual reproduction helps a species to survive.

Sexual reproduction leads to variations within a species. Gradually, favourable characteristics are selected, and evolution takes place.

Sexual reproduction involves the exchange and interaction of genetic material, which gives rise to variations within a species.

4. B

The lobe characteristic is an inherited genetic trait. The trait acquired is either the dominant free lobe trait or the recessive attached lobe trait. Such a trait is heritable with a distinct or discrete variation.

NR 1   2143

The male sperm and the female egg are gametes (2) that unite in the process of fertilization (1) to produce a zygote (4). The zygote, through the process of cell division, develops into an embryo (3) and eventually into a new individual.

5. C

The pollen or male gamete is produced in the anther. The fine grains of pollen drop onto the stigma of the pistil and travel through the style into the ovary, where fertilization takes place.

6. D

Amoebas do not show genetic variation within each species because there is no exchange of genetic information by sexual reproduction. Amoebas only reproduce asexually, which means that the daughter cells are exact duplicates of the parent cells.

Various combinations of genes in sexual reproduction produce a wide range of variation within a species. Sexual reproduction requires specialized cells called gametes. These are the male sperm and the female egg. Fertilization in sexual reproduction requires a tremendous amount of energy. In asexual reproduction, the individual takes on the characteristics of the parent individual. It is an exact clone.

7. D

DNA contains the instructional material for an organism's traits. This genetic material is carried in the chromosome part of the nucleus.
The cytoplasm is the semi-liquid contents of the cell. The cell wall is the protective layer through which water and nutrients pass. Chloroplasts function in the process of photosynthesis.

8. A

Meiosis is the division of sex cells. Because meiosis is a double division, it produces 23 chromosomes. Mitosis is the division of body cells and always produces 46 chromosomes in humans.

9. D

An embryo developing from a zygote involves the fertilization of male and female gametes. This is sexual reproduction.

10. B

The association of a bee and a clusia flower is an example of mutualism. In mutualism, both partners in the association are mutually benefited by each other. The bee carries out pollination, and in turn, it gets the antibiotic that kills the bacteria in its hive. In parasitism, the host is harmed, and in commensalism, the host is unaffected. Heterotrophism means depending on others for food.

11. C

Variation within a species is what enables species to survive a changing environment. Some of the individuals will be better suited to the new environment, which will allow those members of the species to survive. If all members are the same, a change in the environment could result in the extinction or extirpation of that species.

12. B

The steps of the DNA ladder are made of nitrogen bases, which are joined together by a hydrogen bond. DNA is a double helical structure composed of a large number of nucleotide molecules. The outer part or upright part consists of deoxyribose sugar and phosphate.

13. D

Uracil is not present in DNA. Uracil is a nitrogen base found in RNA. DNA is a giant molecule composed of nucleotide molecules. Each nucleotide contains deoxyibose sugar, phosphates, and a pair of nitrogen bases: adenine and thiamine or guanine and cytosine.

14. B

Tropical rain forests are found in equatorial regions. These regions are some of the oldest, most climatically undisturbed areas on Earth. The organisms within this biome have adapted well to the hot, humid conditions. Tropical rainforests support a large diverse population of living things.

15. C

The main drawback to using hybridized species is that the genetic diversity is decreased. Biodiversity is very important in maintaining healthy and viable ecosystems and populations.

1. *What is the difference between artificial selection and natural selection?*

Natural selection is a process by which the environment selects which individuals will survive and reproduce.

Artificial selection is the process by which humans select the most desirable traits in order to produce offspring with these traits.

2. *Describe the difference between an endangered species and an extinct species, and give an example of each.*

An endangered species is on the verge of extinction; that is, there are very few left. An example is the whooping crane. An extinct species has totally disappeared, and there are none left. An example is the passenger pigeon.

3. *Indicate two human factors that have contributed to the loss of biodiversity in the prairie area of Alberta.*

Any two of the following:

- Loss of habitat as a result of clearing and draining of land for agricultural purposes.

- Loss of habitat as a result of oil and gas exploration

- Loss of habitat as a result of urban expansion

- Loss of species as a result of excessive use of pesticides

NOTES

MATTER AND CHEMICAL CHANGE

<table>
<thead>
<tr>
<th colspan="4">Table of Correlations</th>
</tr>
<tr>
<th>Specific Expectation</th>
<th>Practice Questions</th>
<th>Unit Test Questions</th>
<th>2006 PAT</th>
</tr>
</thead>
<tbody>
<tr>
<td colspan="4">Students will:</td>
</tr>
<tr>
<td colspan="4">B.1.   Investigate materials, and describe them in terms of their physical and chemical properties</td>
</tr>
<tr>
<td>B.1.1 investigate and describe properties of materials</td>
<td>1, 11</td>
<td>1</td>
<td></td>
</tr>
<tr>
<td>B.1.2 describe and apply different ways of classifying materials based on their composition and properties, including:
• distinguishing between pure substances, solutions and mechanical mixtures
• distinguishing between metals and non-metals
• identifying and applying other methods of classification</td>
<td>4, 5, 6</td>
<td>2, 3</td>
<td></td>
</tr>
<tr>
<td>B.1.3 identify conditions under which properties of a material are changed, and critically evaluate if a new substance has been produced</td>
<td>2, 3, 7</td>
<td></td>
<td>13</td>
</tr>
<tr>
<td colspan="4">B.2.   Describe and interpret patterns in chemical reactions</td>
</tr>
<tr>
<td>B.2.1 identify and evaluate dangers of caustic materials and potentially explosive reactions</td>
<td>8, 9</td>
<td>NR1, 4</td>
<td>NR2</td>
</tr>
<tr>
<td>B.2.2 observe and describe evidence of chemical change in reactions between familiar materials, by:
• describing combustion, corrosion and other reactions involving oxygen
• observing and inferring evidence of chemical reactions between familiar household materials</td>
<td>10</td>
<td>8</td>
<td></td>
</tr>
<tr>
<td>B.2.3 distinguish between materials that react readily and those that do not</td>
<td>11, 12</td>
<td></td>
<td></td>
</tr>
<tr>
<td>B.2.4 observe and describe patterns of chemical change by:
• observing heat generated or absorbed in chemical reactions, and identifying examples of exothermic and endothermic reactions
• identifying conditions that affect rates of reactions
• identifying evidence for conservation of mass in chemical reactions, and demonstrating and describing techniques by which that evidence is gathered.</td>
<td>13, 14, 15</td>
<td>5, 9, WR1</td>
<td>18, 19, 20</td>
</tr>
</tbody>
</table>

B.3.	Describe ideas used in interpreting the chemical nature of matter, both in the past and present, and identify example evidence that has contributed to the development of these ideas			
B.3.1 demonstrate understanding of the origins of the periodic table, and relate patterns in the physical and chemical properties of elements to their positions in the periodic table—focusing on the first 18 elements	19, 20	11	16	
B.3.2 distinguish between observation and theory, and provide examples of how models and theoretical ideas are used in explaining observations	17	WR 3		
B.3.3 use the periodic table to identify the number of protons, electrons, and other information about each atom; and describe, in general terms, the relationship between the structure of atoms in each group and the properties of elements in that group	NR1, 16, 18, 21	6, 12, WR2	15	
B.3.4 distinguish between ionic and molecular compounds, and describe the properties of some common examples of each	22, 23	NR2	17	
B.4.	Apply simplified chemical nomenclature in describing elements, compounds, and chemical reactions			
B.4.1 read and interpret chemical formulas for compounds of two elements, and give the IUPAC (International Union of Pure and Applied Chemistry) name and common name of these compounds	24, 25, 28	7, 10	11, 12, 14	
B.4.2 identify/describe chemicals commonly found in the home, and write the chemical symbols	26, 27			
B.4.3 identify examples of combining ratios/number of atoms per molecule found in some common materials, and use information on ion charges to predict combining ratios in ionic compounds of two elements	29			
B.4.4 assemble or draw simple models of molecular and ionic compounds	30, 31			
B.4.5 describe familiar chemical reactions, and represent these reactions by using word equations and chemical formulas and by constructing models of reactants and products	32, 33			

MATTER AND CHEMICAL CHANGE

B.1.1   *investigate and describe properties of materials*

B.1.3   *identify conditions under which properties of a material are changed, and critically evaluate if a new substance has been produced*

B.2.2   *observe and describe evidence of chemical change in reactions between familiar materials, by:*
  - *describing combustion, corrosion, and other reactions involving oxygen*
  - *observing and inferring evidence of chemical reactions between familiar household materials*

MATTER

Matter can be defined as anything that has mass and occupies space. Matter can be identified by its physical and chemical properties. **Physical properties** are easily observable and include characteristics such as melting point, density, colour, and state. **Chemical properties** refer to how the substance reacts with other substances. For example, iron is a reddish solid (physical properties) that reacts with oxygen to form rust (chemical property).

Matter cannot be created or destroyed, but it can undergo change.

Physical changes can be made by altering the following properties of matter:

- State—melting, freezing, boiling, or condensing

- Shape—cutting, breaking, or crushing

- Colour—dying or painting

A physical change occurs when matter changes its shape or state but retains its physical properties, or identity. For example, freezing water to make ice simply changes the water's form. A change of state is a physical change. A physical change does not change the substance into another material. Ice is another form of water. It is not a new material. Another characteristic of a physical change is that it can be reversed. Ice can melt to form liquid water. It can then be frozen to make ice again. Another example of a physical change is when large pieces of copper are heated and stretched into copper wire. During the change, the copper changes its physical appearance but keeps its identity. The type of matter has not changed, but its shape has.

A chemical change is a change in matter that produces one or more new substances. The new substance has properties that are different from the properties of the starting materials. For example, fire is created when oxygen and wood react in the presence of heat. Ash and smoke are new substances created when wood is burned. It is important to note that a chemical change cannot always be reversed. You cannot take ash from a fire and turn it back into wood.

Another example occurs when you apply heat to a raw egg. The egg cooks. The heat has caused a chemical change, and you cannot uncook the egg.

How can you tell when a chemical change or a chemical reaction has occurred? Scientists look for the following signs, or evidence, of a chemical change:

- A gas is produced.

- A substance disappears.

- A solid is formed.

- Heat is given off.

- A smell is produced.

A good example of a chemical reaction is what happens when you take a tablespoon of baking soda and mix it into a cup of vinegar. You will see a lot of bubbles and foam forming. These bubbles and foam are evidence of a chemical reaction. The gas that is produced in the bubbles and foam is called carbon dioxide.

A physical change does not affect the type of matter, but it will result in the matter having different physical properties. On the other hand, a chemical change will produce new matter with different characteristics from the original matter.

Practice Questions: 1, 2, 3, 7, 10, 11

B.1.2   *describe and apply different ways of classifying materials based on their composition and properties, including:*
  * *distinguishing between pure substances, solutions, and mechanical mixtures*
  * *distinguishing between metals and non-metals*
  * *identifying and applying other methods of classification*

CLASSIFYING MATTER

Scientists have divided the types of matter into subcategories based on distinct characteristics and properties. Remember that all matter exists as a solid, a liquid, or a gas.

As well, all matter can be classified as a pure substance or a mixture.

There are two types of pure substances: elements and compounds. There are two types of mixtures: heterogeneous and homogeneous.

Heterogeneous mixtures can be further classified into three other types:

• Mechanical mixtures

• Suspensions

• Colloids (including emulsions)

There is only one type of homogeneous mixture: solutions.

The following flow chart shows how matter is organized and classified.

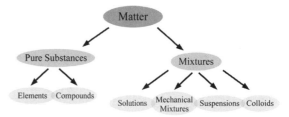

A **pure substance** cannot be broken down into simpler substances by physical means. A **mixture**, however, can be separated into component parts by physical means, such as filtration. Pure substances are grouped into **elements**, which are substances composed of only one kind of atom, and **compounds**, which are substances composed of two or more elements that are chemically combined. Hydrogen, oxygen, and gold are examples of elements. Water and sugar are examples of compounds. Compounds can only be separated by a chemical reaction.

A common method of classifying matter is by separating it into metals and non-metals. Substances that are classified as metals generally are shiny, malleable, ductile, and electrical conductors. Iron, copper and aluminum are metals. Non-metals are dull, brittle, and do not conduct electricity. Examples of non-metals are oxygen, phosphorous, and sulfur.

Practice Questions: 4, 5, 6

B.2.1   identify and evaluate dangers of caustic materials and potentially explosive reactions

B.2.3   distinguish between materials that react readily and those that do not

CHEMICAL SAFETY

Chemical reactions provide many benefits to society; they are used in the creation of useful compounds and in the processing of many different materials. A solid understanding of the reactions involved is required to avoid and minimize potential safety and environmental issues. For example, both ammonia and chlorine bleach are used as household cleaning agents. If the two substances are mixed, they produce highly toxic chlorine gas.

The Workplace Hazardous Materials Information System (WHMIS) is a system created to reduce the number of safety and environmental issues that can arise as a result of chemical reactions.

The eight WHMIS symbols and what they represent are as follows:

Compressed Gas — Flammable and Combustible Material — Oxidizing Material — Poisonous Materials Causing Immediate and Serious Toxic Effects

  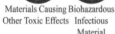

Materials Causing Other Toxic Effects — Biohazardous Infectious Material — Corrosive Material — Dangerously Reactive Material

Practice Questions: 8, 9, 11, 12

B.2.4   observe and describe patterns of chemical change, by:

- *observing heat generated or absorbed in chemical reactions, and identifying examples of exothermic and endothermic reactions*
- *identifying conditions that affect rates of reactions*
- *identifying evidence for conservation of mass in chemical reactions, and demonstrating and describing techniques by which that evidence is gathered.*

B.4.5   describe familiar chemical reactions, and represent these reactions by using word equations and chemical formulas and by constructing models of reactants and products

CHEMICAL REACTIONS

In a chemical reaction, the starting materials, which are called **reactants**, react to create new materials called **products**. The law of conservation of mass states that the mass of the reactants equals the mass of the products. Matter is neither created nor destroyed; it is only changed.

Chemical reactions can be represented in word equation form or in symbol equation form.

The reaction of magnesium in hydrochloric acid can be written in the following two ways.

Word equation
Magnesium reacts with hydrochloric acid to produce magnesium chloride and hydrogen gas.

Symbol equation
$$Mg_{(s)} + 2HCl_{(aq)} \rightarrow MgCl_{2(aq)} + H_{2(g)}$$
REACTANTS   PRODUCTS

The balanced symbol equation shows that the reaction conforms to the law of conservation of matter. The total number of atoms on the reactant side is equal to the total number of atoms on the product side.

One way of classifying chemical reactions is by whether they release or absorb heat. A reaction that releases heat is known as **exothermic**, while a reaction that absorbs heat is called **endothermic**.

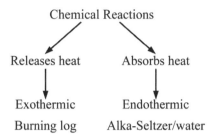

Different reactions occur at different rates. For example, some oxidation reactions, which involve oxygen and are common in nature, are very rapid, while others are very slow. When fuel is burned in a car, the reaction happens quickly to produce carbon dioxide and water vapour. A much slower oxidation reaction is rusting, which is an example of corrosion.

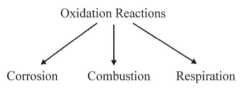

The rate of a chemical reaction can be increased or decreased by the following factors:

• Introducing a catalyst

• Changing the temperature

• Changing the surface area

• Changing the concentration

Practice Questions: 13, 14, 15, 32, 33

B.3.2 *distinguish between observation and theory, and provide examples of how models and theoretical ideas are used in explaining observations*

SCIENTIFIC THEORY

A scientific theory is a set of ideas that help to explain certain facts. A theory is not a guess; it is an explanation that has been tested and is supported by the results of experiments. A theory is accepted to be correct according to the information that is available at the time.

However, theories can be disproved as new information becomes available or as technology improves. As more scientific knowledge is gained, existing theories are challenged or re-evaluated. When an accepted theory is disproved and no longer explains certain facts, scientists develop a new theory to explain the available information.

A good example of how new discoveries and technology change theories is the development of the atomic theory. The atomic theory originated with the ancient Greeks and continues to develop today.

GENERAL TIMELINE OF ATOMIC THEORY

Around 400 BC, the Greek philosopher Democritus used the word *atomos* to describe the smallest particles of matter that could not be broken down any further. The Greek word *atomos* means indivisible.

In the 1660s, Robert Boyle studied the properties of gases. He believed that all matter was made up of tiny particles and that these particles combined to make different substances.

John Dalton suggested that all matter is made up of elements in 1808. He was the first to suggest that these elements are pure substances made of particles called **atoms**. Dalton believed that atoms were tiny, solid spheres of matter.

J. Plücker built a cathode ray tube in 1859. The cathode ray tube would be used by others to study gas molecules in more detail.

In 1897, J.J. Thompson used a cathode ray tube to show that the cathode rays were made of negatively charged particles. He called these particles electrons, and he showed that these particles were much smaller than atoms.
He described the raisin-bun model of the atom. This model had a large positive particle in the centre, with small, negative electrons stuck around the outside of it.

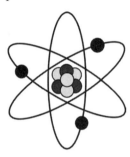

Hantaro Nagaoka introduced the Saturn model of the atom in 1904. This model had a central positive charge and the electrons orbiting around the centre like planets around the sun.

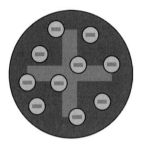

In 1911, Ernest Rutherford projected positively charged particles through thin gold foil.
He suggested that the nucleus was both very small and positively charged. Rutherford also believed that the electrons were located outside the nucleus.

In 1914, Henry Gwyn Jeffreys Moseley used X-ray tubes to determine that the atomic number of an element was the same as the number of protons in the nucleus. As a result, the periodic table was reorganized according to the atomic numbers of elements instead of their atomic masses.

In 1922, Niels Bohr suggested that electrons do not orbit the nucleus randomly. He showed that they orbit the nucleus in specific shells around it.

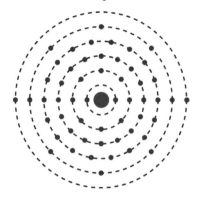

In 1930, Erwin Schrodinger described the movement of electrons as forming continuous clouds around the nucleus.

In 1968, it was shown that the nucleus contains particles smaller than either protons or neutrons. These particles were called quarks.

From 1978 to 1995, several experiments confirmed the existence of quarks. Researchers also tried to measure some of the properties of quarks.

From 1995 to today, nuclear physicists have continued to explore the properties of the nuclei of different elements.

As you can see from this timeline of the development of atomic theory, scientific knowledge is always changing. As more information is found and technology continues to develop, scientists continue to re-evaluate accepted theories in order to explain the new information.

Practice Question: 17

*B.3.1   demonstrate understanding of the origins
of the periodic table, and relate patterns
in the physical and chemical properties of
elements to their positions in the periodic
table—focusing on the first 18 elements*

THE PERIODIC TABLE

HISTORY AND TRENDS

Matter has been studied for many centuries.
In the late 1800s, Dmitri Mendeleev organized the
elements into the periodic table. The periodic
table is separated by a staircase, with metals on the
left of the staircase and non-metals on the right.
Metals have some similarities in their chemical
properties because they all lose electrons to form
positive ions. Typically, metals are shiny,
flexible, and good conductors of heat and
electricity. Almost all metals are solids at room
temperature and normal pressure. Non-metals are
to the right of the staircase. The chemical
properties of non-metals are related to the fact that
they accept electrons to form negative ions.
Physically, non-metals are typically poor
conductors of heat and electricity. They can be
solids, liquids, or gases at normal temperature
and pressure.

Each horizontal row of the periodic table is called
a **period**. The period of an element is determined
by the number of energy levels that are occupied
by electrons. Each vertical column of the periodic
table is a **group**, or family. All the members of a
chemical group have similar chemical properties.
That is, they react with the same elements in a
similar way. Group 1, the alkali metals, all have
one valence electron and are all highly reactive
metals. Group 2, the alkaline-earth metals, can all
combine by ionic bonding with two atoms of
members of Group 17 ($BeCl_2$, $MgCl_2$, $CaCl_2$, etc.).
Group 17, the most reactive non-metals, are called
the halogens. Group 18, the noble gases, do not
have any unpaired electrons in their valence
energy levels. They are inert and do not react to
form compounds under normal circumstances.

Practice Questions: 19, 20

*B.3.3   use the periodic table to identify the
number of protons, electrons, and other
information about each atom; and
describe, in general terms, the
relationship between the structure of
atoms in each group and the properties of
elements in that group*

ATOMIC STRUCTURE AND THE PROPERTIES OF ELEMENTS

Atoms are composed of three basic subatomic
particles: protons, electrons, and neutrons
(acronym PEN). Each of these particles is
identified by specific characteristics.

Particle	Proton	Electron	Neutron
Charge	+ Positive	– Negative	No charge
Size	Large—same as a neutron	Small—about $\frac{1}{2000}$ the size of the proton	Large—same as a proton
Location	Nucleus	Cloud around nucleus	Nucleus

The **atomic number** of an atom is the number of
protons found in the nucleus. This also represents
the number of electrons found in the orbits. The
elements in the periodic table are arranged in order
of increasing atomic number. For example, the
first element is hydrogen, which has one proton
and an atomic number of 1. The second element is
helium, which has two protons and an atomic
number of 2, and so on.

The **atomic mass unit** (amu) of an atom is
the total mass of the protons and neutrons in
the nucleus.

This information can be found for each element in
the periodic table.

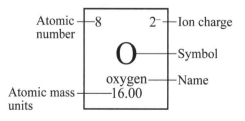

Oxygen has an atomic number of eight. This means that there are eight protons and eight electrons in an oxygen atom. The mass of oxygen is 16.00 amu. You can calculate the number of neutrons by subtracting the atomic number from the mass number.

$$\frac{Mass}{number} - \frac{Atomic}{number} = \frac{Number}{of\ neutrons}$$

For oxygen, the number of neutrons can be calculated as follows:
$16.00 - 8 = 8$ neutrons

Practice Questions: NR1, 16, 18, 21

B.3.4   distinguish between ionic and molecular compounds, and describe the properties of some common examples of each

IONIC AND MOLECULAR COMPOUNDS

Atoms of different elements can join together to form compounds. Recall that the periodic table can be divided into metals on the left side of the staircase and non-metals on the right side of the staircase. When a metal and a non-metal are joined together, they are joined by an ionic bond, and the resulting compound is called an **ionic compound**. An example of an ionic compound is sodium chloride, $NaCl_{(s)}$, also known as table salt. Sodium atoms (metal) are joined by ionic bonds to chlorine atoms (non-metal). All ionic compounds are solids at room temperature and have relatively high melting points. They have distinct crystal structures and can conduct electricity if they have been melted or dissolved in water.

Bonds can also form between two different non-metals. This is called covalent bonding, and the compounds that are formed are called **molecular compounds**.

One of the most common examples of a covalently bonded molecular compound is water, $H_2O_{(l)}$. Table sugar, $C_{12}H_{22}O_{11(s)}$, is another example of a molecular compound. Several elements are able to form covalent molecules using only their own atoms. Hydrogen, fluorine, and oxygen atoms are found in nature as pairs of atoms. For this reason, they are called diatomic elements.

Molecular compounds can be solids, liquids, or gases at room temperature. They generally do not conduct electricity, and they have relatively low melting and boiling points because the bonds holding them together are much weaker than those in ionic compounds.

Practice Questions: 22, 23

B.4.1   read and interpret chemical formulas for compounds of two elements, and give the IUPAC (International Union of Pure and Applied Chemistry) name and common name of these compounds

CHEMICAL FORMULAS

For ease of communication, the International Union of Pure and Applied Chemistry, IUPAC, has developed a system for naming chemical compounds. The IUPAC rules state that for the names of ionic compounds, the metal is named first. The non-metal is written second, and its name is changed so that it ends in the suffix –ide. The exception to this rule is if the non-metal is a polyatomic ion. In that case, the name does not change to end in –ide.

For example, AlN is named aluminum nitride, and $MgCl_2$ is named magnesium chloride.

Sometimes, a metal can have more than one possible ion charge. For example, copper can have a charge of 2+ or 1+. When naming an ionic compound, it needs to be clear which ion is being used. For that reason, a roman numeral is added to the chemical name. For example, copper(II) chloride is a compound that contains a Cu^{2+} ion, and copper(I) chloride is a compound that contains a Cu^{1+} ion.

Unlike ionic compounds, molecular compounds use prefixes to show how many atoms of each element are present.

Number of Atoms	Prefix
1	Mono-
2	Di-
3	Tri-
4	Tetra-
5	Penta-

Molecular compounds are named using the following rule:

Prefix + first element
prefix + second element (ending in –ide)

Note: If the first element only has one atom, the prefix mono- is not used.

Example

$N_2O_3 \rightarrow$ *dinitrogen trioxide*

$CCl_4 \rightarrow$ *carbon tetrachloride*

Some compounds also have common names. For example, the chemical formula H_2O would be named according to IUPAC rules as dihydrogen monoxide. This compound is more commonly referred to by its common name, water.

Practice Questions: 24, 28

B.4.2   identify/describe chemicals commonly found in the home, and write the chemical symbols

COMMON HOUSEHOLD CHEMICALS

There are ionic and molecular compounds all around you. Even in your home, there are many compounds you use frequently. The following table outlines some common chemical compounds, their formulas, common names, and compound type.

Name	Formula	Ionic or Molecular
Baking soda	$NaHCO_{3(s)}$	Ionic
Salt	$NaCl_{(s)}$	Ionic
Water	$H_2O_{(l)}$	Molecular
Table sugar	$C_{12}H_{22}O_{11(s)}$	Molecular
Rubbing alcohol	$C_3H_8O_{(l)}$	Molecular
Hydrogen peroxide	$H_2O_{2(l)}$	Molecular

Practice Questions: 26, 27

B.4.3   identify examples of combining ratios/number of atoms per molecule found in some common materials, and use information on ion charges to predict combining ratios in ionic compounds of two elements

PREDICT COMBINING RATIOS FOR IONIC COMPOUNDS

If you know the chemical name and the ion charges of a compound, you can write its chemical formula. First, write the metal element's symbol with the ion charge. Next to it, write the non-metal element's symbol and charge. Remember that ion charges are found in the periodic table and are written as **superscripts**. The net charge of the compound must be zero, so the positive charges must be balanced with the negative charges.

In the following example, you will see that there must be two chlorine ions, each with a charge of 1– to balance out the 2+ charge of the magnesium ion. Finally, write the formula, using **subscripts** to indicate how many atoms of each element are present. Do not include the ion charges in this step. Note that if only one atom is present, no subscripts are used.

Example

Magnesium chloride

- Mg^{2+} Cl^{1-}

- Mg^{2+} Cl^{1-} Cl^{1-}

. $MgCl_{2(s)}$

Practice Questions: 29

B.4.4 assemble or draw simple models of molecular and ionic compounds

DRAWING MOLECULAR AND IONIC COMPOUNDS

Many of the common substances you use every day are made up of simple compounds. To get a better understanding of these compounds, scientists build models of them. These models are useful because they represent what a molecule would look like if you were able to see it. The model can reveal useful information about a molecule by showing how many atoms of each element are present and how they are arranged.

For example, the chemical formula for water is H_2O. The letters represent elements found on the periodic table. The subscript number after the letter indicates how many atoms of that particular element are present in the compound. If no number is found after an element, it means there is only one atom of that element present. For water, the first letter, H, represents hydrogen. The subscript, 2, that comes after H indicates there are two hydrogen atoms present. The O represents oxygen. No number is found after the O, which indicates that only one atom of oxygen is present.

To draw a molecule of water, simply place the oxygen in the centre, and attach the two hydrogen molecules to it.

Ammonia has the chemical formula NH_3. There is one nitrogen atom surrounded by three hydrogen atoms.

Carbon dioxide, CO_2, can be drawn in the following manner:

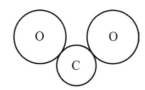

Practice Questions: 30, 31

PRACTICE QUESTIONS—MATTER AND CHEMICAL CHANGE

1. Which of the following characteristics does **not** apply to water?

   A. It is a good solvent.

   B. It forms crystals in a solid form.

   C. It is colourless at room temperature.

   D. It is a solid, a liquid, or a gas at room temperature.

2. Which of the following changes is an example of a physical change?

   A. Melting ice

   B. Rusting iron

   C. Burning paper

   D. Photosynthesis

Use the following information to answer the next question.

Isabella watched her mother crack eggs into a frying pan. She noticed that the transparent liquid surrounding the yolks of the eggs became solid and white when the pan was placed over the burner of the stove.

3. Which of the following statements **best** describes the changes that occur to the egg during frying?

   A. The changes are physical because a change in state occurs and an odour is detected.

   B. The changes are chemical because heat is absorbed and a new substance is formed.

   C. The changes are chemical because an odour is detected and heat is released.

   D. The changes are physical because a new colour appears and heat is absorbed.

Use the following information to answer the next question.

Cement and gravel are combined in specific proportions to produce concrete.

4. The combination of cement and gravel is known as

   A. an alloy

   B. a solution

   C. a pure substance

   D. a mechanical mixture

Use the following information to answer the next question.

A difference between a compound and a mixture is that a compound __*i*__ and a mixture __*ii*__ .

5. This statement is completed by the information in which of the following rows?

Row	*i*	*ii*
A.	is made of elements	is not made of elements
B.	has properties that are always the same	does not have properties that are always the same
C.	can dissolve	cannot dissolve
D.	is colourless	is visible

Use the following information to answer the next question.

A very long time ago, it was discovered that tin and copper could be combined to make bronze. Bronze is stronger and more durable than either tin or copper.

6. Bronze is an example of
    A. an alloy
    B. an element
    C. a pure substance
    D. a mechanical mixture

Use the following information to answer the next question.

Juan rubbed an iron nail with a strong magnet. After placing the magnetized nail on a wet tabletop, he observed reddish-brown spots appearing on the nail.

7. The changes Juan observed in magnetizing and then placing the magnet on wet surface are examples of a
    A. chemical change and a chemical change, respectively
    B. physical change and a chemical change, respectively
    C. chemical change and a physical change, respectively
    D. physical change and a physical change, respectively

Use the following information to answer the next question.

WHMIS label on a bottle containing a chemical

8. The liquid in the given bottle is **most likely**
    A. corrosive
    B. flammable
    C. an oxidizing agent
    D. dangerously reactive

Use the following information to answer the next question.

During his yearly spring cleaning, Kyle came across four containers marked with WHMIS symbols.

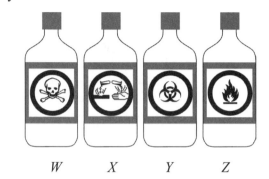

W   X   Y   Z

9. Which of the given containers should be kept away from an open flame?

   A. *W*

   B. *X*

   C. *Y*

   D. *Z*

Use the following information to answer the next question.

iron + water + oxygen → rust

10. The given chemical reaction is an example of

   A. corrosion

   B. combustion

   C. neutralization

   D. decomposition

11. Which of the following characteristics describes a property of metals?

   A. Dull

   B. Brittle

   C. Malleable

   D. Poor electrical conductor

Use the following information to answer the next question.

As part of a science project, Theo performed four chemical reaction experiments by mixing reactants in a test tube.

Test Tube	Reactant 1	Reactant 2
1	Steel wool (iron)	Oxygen/water
2	Vinegar	Baking soda
3	Magnesium strip	Hydrochloric acid
4	Alka-Seltzer tablet	Water

CHALLENGER QUESTION

12. If a lit splint were placed over the mouth of each test tube, which of the given reactions would be the **most dangerous**?

   A. 1

   B. 2

   C. 3

   D. 4

*Use the following information to answer
the next question.*

A scientist found the mass of two samples of chemical compounds. The scientist placed the two compounds into a beaker and observed the resulting chemical reaction. The scientist then found the mass of the product in the beaker. The final mass was less than the mass of the two original samples.

13. The **most likely** explanation for the difference in mass is that

    A. one product of the reaction was a gas that escaped into the air

    B. part of the original mass was converted to heat

    C. the scientist made an error in measurement

    D. the product was hot, resulting in less mass

Source: PAT, 1999

14. The hydrogen that scientists produce can be burned to generate electricity. The burning of hydrogen is

    A. an endothermic reaction

    B. a neutralization reaction

    C. an exothermic reaction

    D. a corrosion reaction

*Use the following information to answer
the next question.*

Frost forms when moisture in the air condenses onto surfaces such as windows. Cold air temperatures cause the condensation to freeze and form white crystals.  During the formation of frost, heat is released into the air.

15. The formation of frost is an example of an

    A. exothermic physical change

    B. exothermic chemical change

    C. endothermic physical change

    D. endothermic chemical change

16. Hydrogen has an atomic number of one, whereas oxygen has an atomic number of eight. This means that each hydrogen atom has

    A. one proton, whereas each oxygen atom has eight protons

    B. one neutron, whereas each oxygen atom has eight neutrons

    C. one energy level, whereas each oxygen atom has eight energy levels

    D. an atomic mass of one, whereas each oxygen atom has an atomic mass of eight

*Use the following information to answer
the next question.*

Modern atomic theory began with the work of John Dalton. He proposed that the atom was the smallest particle of matter and was therefore indivisible. Later, through the work of J.J. Thomson, subatomic particles known as electrons were discovered, and atomic theory changed to take into account the presence of particles smaller than an atom.

17. What does the given case illustrate about the evolution of scientific knowledge?

    A. Scientific knowledge has remained largely unchanged.

    B. Scientific knowledge is largely gained by chance in laboratories.

    C. Scientific knowledge is constantly changing or being modified.

    D. Scientific knowledge can only progress if more than one scientist investigates the idea.

Use the following information to answer the next question.

The information box from the periodic table for the metal sodium is shown.

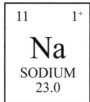

11	1⁺
Na	
SODIUM	
23.0	

18. How many neutrons does a sodium atom have?

A. 11

B. 12

C. 23

D. 24

Use the following information to answer the next three questions.

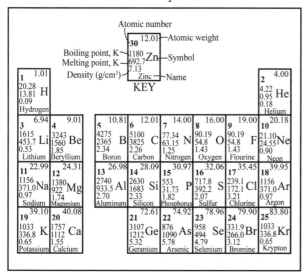

19. Which of the following elements becomes a solid at the lowest temperature?

A. Hydrogen

B. Oxygen

C. Helium

D. Neon

Numerical Response

1. The total mass of one molecule of water (H_2O) is _____ amu.
(Record your answer to **two** decimal places.)

Use the following additional information to answer the next question.

The column on the far right of the periodic table is a group of elements known as the noble gases. These elements include He, Ne, Ar, and Kr.

20. What is one way in which the noble gases differ from other elements?

A. Noble gases have low boiling points.

B. Noble gases have high melting points.

C. Noble gases have extremely high densities.

D. Noble gases have unusually high atomic masses.

21. What does the atomic number of an element indicate?

A. The number of protons and the number of electrons in an atom

B. The number of neutrons in an atom

C. The number of protons in an atom

D. The mass of an atom

22. Ionic compounds display which of the following characteristics?

A. They can be solids, liquids, or gases at room temperature.

B. They have relatively low melting points.

C. They are good conductors of electricity.

D. They are malleable and ductile.

23. The placement of metal and non-metal elements in the periodic table makes it possible to predict the formation of compounds. Which of the following chemical formulas indicates the formation of an ionic compound?

A. KI

B. ICl

C. SO_3

D. $CHCl_3$

24. What are the formulas for iron(II) oxide and iron(III) oxide, respectively?

A. FeO and Fe_2O_3

B. Fe_2O, and Fe_3O_2

C. FeO_2, and Fe_2O_4

D. Fe_2O_2, and Fe_3O_4

25. The formula for copper(II) nitrate is

A. $CuNO_2$

B. Cu_2NO_3

C. $Cu(II)N_2$

D. $Cu(NO_3)_2$

Use the following information to answer the next question.

Glucose sugar, a product of plant photosynthesis, is chemically represented as $C_6H_{12}O_6$. Glucose has __*i*__ elements and a total of __*ii*__ atoms.

26. This statement is completed by the information in which of the following rows?

Row	*i*	*Ii*
A.	3	8
B.	6	12
C.	3	24
D.	6	18

27. What is the chemical formula of baking soda?

A. $CaCO_3$

B. Na_2CO_3

C. $Ca(OH)_2$

D. $NaHCO_3$

28. The chemical formula for aluminum oxide is

A. Al_2

B. AlO

C. AlO_3

D. Al_2O_3

29. Iron combines with oxygen to form rust, which is iron(III) oxide (Fe_2O_3). What are the charges of the iron ion and the oxygen ion, respectively?

A. Fe^{3+}, O^{2-}

B. Fe^{2+}, O^{3-}

C. Fe^{3+}, O^-

D. Fe^{2+}, O^-

30. Which of the following illustrations represents the molecular compound carbon disulfide?

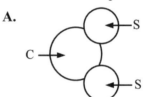

A.

B.

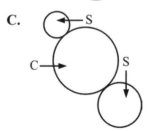

C.

D.

31. Methane gas (also called natural gas) is used as the source of fuel for furnaces in homes. Its chemical formula is CH_4. Which of the following molecular representations **most accurately** represents methane gas?

A.

H_2
|
C
|
H_2

B.

C—H_2

C.

H— C
|
H_3

D.

H
|
H— C—H
|
H

Use the following information to answer the next question.

The voodoo lily, *Sauromatum guttatum*, relies on flies for pollination. To attract flies, the flower emits an odour similar to that of rotting meat. Heat generated by special structures within the plant creates the pungent smell. Mitochondria within these structures produce heat during respiration.

32. In order for the voodoo lily to generate heat, its mitochondria would require

A. oxygen and glucose

B. light and carbon dioxide

C. carbon dioxide and water

D. chloroplasts and ribosomes

Use the following information to answer the next question.

Milk of magnesia (magnesium hydroxide) is used to neutralize excess stomach acid (hydrochloric acid) to prevent heartburn. The products of this reaction are magnesium chloride and water.

33. Which chemical equation represents this reaction?

A. $Mg(OH)_2 + HCl_2 \rightarrow MgCl + H_2O$

B. $MgCl_2 + H_2O \rightarrow MgOH_2 + 2HCl$

C. $Mg(OH)_2 + HCl \rightarrow Mg_2Cl + H_2O$

D. $Mg(OH)_2 + HCl \rightarrow MgCl_2 + H_2O$

ANSWERS AND SOLUTIONS—PRACTICE QUESTIONS

1. D	9. D	17. C	24. A	32. A
2. A	10. A	18. B	25. D	33. D
3. B	11. C	19. C	26. C	
4. D	12. C	NR1. 18.02	27. D	
5. B	13. A	20. A	28. D	
6. A	14. C	21. C	29. A	
7. B	15. A	22. C	30. B	
8. C	16. A	23. A	31. D	

1. D

Unless there are extremely unusual levels of pressure, water is always liquid at room temperature. Water is a good solvent, it forms crystals as a solid, and it is colourless.

2. A

A physical change is easily reversible and does not involve the formation of a new form of matter. The melting of ice is easily reversible and does not result in a new compound.

3. B

When an egg is fried, it undergoes a chemical change because a new substance with new properties is formed. This is not reversible. For example, if you remove the added heat by putting the egg in the refrigerator, it will not return to its original state.

4. D

A mechanical mixture is a mixture of two or more substances. The addition of the gravel to the cement strengthens the mixture by making it harder.

5. B

The properties of a compound such as water are always the same, whereas the properties of a mixture can vary. For example, the strength of concrete can vary depending on how much cement is mixed with the gravel.

6. A

Because bronze is composed of the two metals tin and copper, it is an alloy.

7. B

Because the magnetizing of the nail can be reversed, it is a physical change. Since rusting from the water is irreversible, it is a chemical change. Therefore, the first change is physical, and the second change is chemical.

8. C

According to the Workplace Hazardous Materials Information System (WHMIS) symbols, the liquid in the given bottle is most likely an oxidizing agent.

9. D

Symbol W represents poisonous material, symbol X represents corrosive material, symbol Y represents biohazardous material, and symbol Z represents flammable material. Material that is marked as being flammable should be kept away from an open flame.

10. A

Corrosion occurs when a metal combines with oxygen to form a metal oxide. The rusting of metal is corrosion.

11. C

Metals are generally shiny, malleable, ductile, and good conductors of electricity. Non-metals are dull, brittle, and poor conductors of electricity.

12. C

Reaction 1 is a slow oxidation reaction that produces rust. This would have no effect on the flame.

Reactions 2 and 4 both produce carbon dioxide gas, which would extinguish the flame.

Reaction 3 produces hydrogen gas, which is extremely explosive.

13. A

You know that the mass of the products of a chemical reaction have the same mass as the reactants. You also know that during a chemical change, the products could be solids, liquids, or gases. If the scientist found the contents of the beaker to have less mass after the reaction, it is most likely that one product of the reaction was a gas that left the beaker.

14. C

An exothermic reaction is one that releases energy. Burning releases energy in the form of heat and light. Therefore, burning is exothermic.

15. A

The formation of frost is a change of state that releases heat to the surroundings. The formation of frost is an exothermic physical change.

16. A

The atomic number reflects the number of protons that are present in the atom. Hydrogen has only one proton in its nucleus, whereas oxygen has eight protons in its nucleus.

17. C

Scientific knowledge is always undergoing changes to reflect new discoveries.

18. B

Sodium has an atomic number of 11. This means it has 11 protons and 11 electrons.

The atomic mass unit of 23 indicates the total mass of the atom, which includes the protons, electrons, and neutrons.

The number of neutrons is determined by subtracting the atomic number from the atomic mass unit.
$23 - 11 = 12$ neutrons

19. C

Helium does not form a solid until 0.95 K ($-272.05°C$). The melting point is found on the left side of the box beneath the atomic number and boiling point.

NR 1   18.02

Atomic mass is normally measured in atomic mass units, or amu. The number in the top right corner of each element's box is the atomic mass. Add the atomic masses of two hydrogen atoms and one oxygen atom to find the atomic mass of one molecule of water.
$1.01 + 1.01 + 16.00 = 18.02$
(2 hydrogen + 1 oxygen)

20. A

The noble gases all have low boiling points, which is why they are always gases under normal conditions.

21. C

The atomic number is the number of protons contained in the nucleus of an atom.

22. C

Ionic compounds are solid at room temperature, have crystal structures, relatively high melting points, and are good conductors of electricity. Conversely, molecular compounds are insulators, can be solids, liquids, or gases at room temperature, and have relatively low melting and boiling points.

23. A

Metal elements have the potential to lose electrons to become positively charged ions. Similarly, non-metal elements gain electrons to become negative ions. Positive and negative ions combine to form ionic compounds. The positive potassium ion combines with the negative iodine ion to form the ionic compound potassium iodide (KI).

24. A

To find the correct formulas, first determine the ion charges. Oxygen has a charge of 2^-. Iron(II) has a charge of 2^+, while iron(III) has a charge of 3^+. The net charge of the compound must be 0. For iron(II) oxide, the ions have charges of 2^+ and 2^-, which, if combined in a 1:1 ratio, will have a net charge of 0. Therefore, the formula will be FeO. Iron(III) oxide will have ions with charges of 3^+ and 2^-, respectively. The lowest common multipliers that result in a net charge of 0 would give the formula Fe_2O_3.

25. D

Copper(II) has a charge of 2^+ (Cu^{2+}). Nitrate can be found on a table of polyatomic ions (NO_3^-). It has a charge of 1^-. It takes one Cu^{2+} to balance two NO_3^-. The formula for copper(II) nitrate is $Cu(NO_3)_2$.

26. C

Glucose has three elements: C (carbon), H (hydrogen), and O (oxygen).

Glucose has six carbon atoms, 12 hydrogen atoms, and six oxygen atoms. Glucose has a total of 24 atoms.
$6 C + 12 H + 6 O = 24$

27. D

Baking soda is sodium hydrogen carbonate. The chemical formula of baking soda is $NaHCO_3$.

28. D

The ion charges for the atoms present are Al^{3+} and O^{2-}. In order for the net charge of the molecule to be zero, there must be $2 \times Al^{3+}$ and $3 \times O^{2-}$. This will combine in a formula as Al_2O_3. Remember that the chemical formula just shows the number of atoms present; the ion charges are not shown.

29. A

Iron oxide is an ionic compound; therefore, the positive and negative charges must balance so that the compound's charge is neutral.

Based on the subscripts, two atoms of iron are used to balance three atoms of oxygen. Iron has a 3+ charge (Fe^{3+}), and oxygen has a 2– charge (O^{2-}).

30. B

Carbon (amu 12) is a smaller atom than sulfur (amu 32). *Di* means two. The two sulfur atoms are the same size, but they are each larger than one carbon atom.

31. D

Carbon generally has four electrons in the outermost ring, which means it has four bonds. Hydrogen has one electron in its last ring, or one bond. Each of the four hydrogen atoms is bonded to the one carbon atom.

32. A

In order to generate heat, the mitochondria of the voodoo lily would have to undergo respiration, which is represented by the following equation:
glucose + oxygen
$\rightarrow$ carbon dioxide + water + heat + ATP

The reactants in cellular respiration are glucose and oxygen.

33. D

The correct chemical formula for each reactant and product must be given. Remember that reactants are found on the left side of the arrow, and products are found on the right. The correct equation for this reaction is given as follows:
$Mg(OH)_2 + HCl \rightarrow MgCl_2 + H_2O$

UNIT TEST—MATTER AND CHEMICAL CHANGE

Use the following information to answer the next question.

Many household products have warning labels on their containers. Hazardous product labels consist of a specific warning symbol outlined by a particular shape, depending on the degree of danger posed by the substance. For example, the corrosive symbol can be outlined by an octagon, a triangle, or a diamond.

1   2   3

Numerical Response

1. When the given symbols are arranged in order from the one that represents the **least corrosive** substance to the one that represents the **most corrosive** substance, the order is ____, ____, and ____. (Record your answer as a **three-digit** number.)

Use the following information to answer the next question.

An unknown substance has the following properties:

I. Solid at room temperature

II. Tarnishes when exposed to air for a period of time

III. Excellent electrical conductor

IV. Malleable

V. Produces bubbling when combined with hydrochloric acid

VI. Has a density of 10.5 g/cm^3

1. How many of the listed properties are physical properties?

   A. 2   **B.** 3

   C. 4   **D.** 5

Use the following information to answer the next question.

The following diagram is a partial classification chart for identifying the structure of matter.

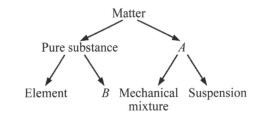

2. The letters *A* and *B* in the chart represent

   A. mixture and colloid, respectively

   B. solution and mixture, respectively

   C. compound and mixture, respectively

   D. mixture and compound, respectively

3. Emulsified liquids, such as homogenized milk, are referred to as

A. aqueous solutions

B. compounds

C. colloids

D. alloys

Use the following information to answer the next question.

An industrial inspector spotted this container outside a delivery door.

4. The inspector informed the delivery people that the container should be handled with care because it contained

A. a corrosive material

B. an oxidizing liquid

C. a compressed gas

D. a flammable gas

Use the following information to answer the next question.

In an experiment, a tablet of the antacid Alka-Seltzer was dropped into a container of water. The temperature of the water was measured every minute for four minutes.

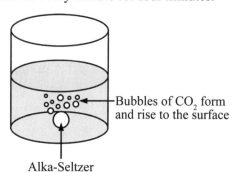

Bubbles of CO_2 form and rise to the surface

Alka-Seltzer

Minute	Temperature (in °C)
0	24.5
1	24.3
2	24.1
3	23.9
4	23.7

5. Given this information, it can be concluded that the Alka-Seltzer tablet underwent a

A. physical state change

B. physical colour change

C. chemical exothermic change

D. chemical endothermic change

Use the following information to answer the next question.

The information box from the periodic table for the metal sodium is shown.

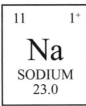

11   1$^+$

Na

SODIUM

23.0

6. How many protons does a sodium atom have?

  A. 11   **B.** 12

  C. 23   **D.** 34

7. The chemical formula for acetylsalicylic acid (Aspirin) is $C_9H_8O_4$. How many elements and atoms are in one molecule of Aspirin?

  A. Twenty-one elements and three atoms

  B. Three elements and three atoms

  C. Three elements and 21 atoms

  D. Nine elements and 21 atoms

8. The chemical reaction that produces rust is called

  A. cellular respiration

  B. conservation

  C. combustion

  D. corrosion

9. A student is given an antacid tablet and a container of mild acid. What could the student do to **best** slow the rate of the reaction that will occur between the tablet and the acid?

  A. Drop the whole tablet into cold acid

  B. Drop the whole tablet into warm acid

  C. Crush the tablet and drop it into cold acid

  D. Crush the tablet and drop it into warm acid

10. The formula for mercury(I) chloride is

  A. PbCl

  B. AuCl

  C. HgCl

  D. MeCl

Use the following information to answer the next question.

The Swedish chemist Jöns Jakob Berzelius suggested that each element in the periodic table be given a one- or two-letter symbol in order to create an international standard. Since many chemists at that time spoke Latin, several of the symbols for elements are derived from Latin. For example, the element that is called tungsten in English is called wolfram in Latin, and therefore, the chemical symbol for tungsten is W. The Latin name for another element is hydragyrum, and its chemical symbol is Hg.

11. What is the English name of the element Hg?

  A. Iron

  B. Mercury

  C. Hafnium

  D. Hydrogen

12. Which of the following elements has physical and chemical properties **most similar** to those of sodium?

  A. Potassium

  B. Calcium

  C. Iodine

  D. Sulfur

Use the following information to answer the next question.

The following chart identifies certain characteristics of chemical compounds.

W	Generally has low melting and boiling points
X	Is a good conductor of electricity
Y	Formed by the union of a metal with a non-metal
Z	Involves the attraction of charged particles

Numerical Response

2. Write the number 1 in the blank if the characteristic refers to an ionic compound, and write the number 2 in the blank if the characteristic refers to a molecular compound.

___ ___ ___ ___
 W   X   Y   Z
(Record your answer as a **four-digit** number.)

Written Response

1. Explain the law of conservation of mass as applied to chemical reactions. Include an example in your response.

(2 marks)

2. What is the difference between the halogen grouping of elements and the noble gas grouping of elements?

(2 marks)

3. Compare Thompson's and Rutherford's contributions to knowledge about the structure of the atom.

(2 marks)

ANSWERS AND SOLUTIONS—UNIT TEST

NR1. 231	**6. A**	**12. A**
1. C	**7. C**	**NR2. 2111**
2. D	**8. D**	**WR1. See Solution**
3. C	**9. A**	**WR2. See Solution**
4. C	**10. C**	**WR3. See Solution**
5. D	**11. B**	

NR 1   231

The triangular shape means caution. The diamond shape means warning, and the octagon shape means danger.

1.   C

A physical property is easily observable. Colour, density, malleability, lustre, melting point, boiling point, state, and electrical conductivity are physical properties. A chemical property describes how a substance reacts with another substance.

I. Solid at room temperature	Physical
II. Tarnishes when exposed to air for a period of time	Chemical
III. Excellent electrical conductor	Physical
IV. Malleable	Physical
V. Produces bubbling when combined with hydrochloric acid	Chemical
VI. Has a density of 10.5 g/cm^3	Physical

2.   D

Matter is defined as anything that has mass and occupies space. It is divided into pure substances and mixtures (*A*). Pure substances are further divided into elements and compounds (*B*).

3.   C

The high-speed shaking that occurs in homogenization causes the fat drops in milk to split into tiny droplets that remain suspended. Since gravity does not cause the fat droplets to settle out of suspension, milk is referred to as a colloid.

4.   C

Compressed gases are stored in cylindrical containers because the cylinder shape can withstand a tremendous amount of pressure. Compressed gas is represented by the following symbol:

5.   D

Fizzing or the formation of bubbles is an indication of that a chemical reaction is occurring. The drop in temperature means that heat is absorbed. The Alka-Selzer underwent a chemical endothermic reaction.

6.   A

Sodium has an atomic number of 11. This means that it has 11 protons.

7.   C

A molecule of Aspirin has three elements (carbon, hydrogen, and oxygen) and 21 atoms (9 C, 8 H, and 4 O).

8. D

The oxidation reaction that forms rust is called corrosion.

9. A

The rate of a chemical reaction is affected by the surface area, concentration, and temperature of a substance. To slow down the rate of reaction, the student could decrease the temperature (cool down the acid) and minimize the surface area (put the whole tablet into the acid).

10. C

Mercury(I) chloride is an ionic compound because it contains a metallic ion (mercury[I]) and a non-metallic ion (chloride). The symbol for the mercury(I) ion is Hg^+, and the symbol for the chloride ion is Cl^-. Since the mercury(I) ion has a charge of 1+ and the chloride ion has a charge of 1−, they will form a compound in a one-to-one ratio in order to maintain a net charge of zero. The symbolic formula for mercury(I) chloride is HgCl.

11. B

The element symbol for mercury is Hg.

12. A

Like sodium, potassium is found in Group 1 of the periodic table. Elements that are found in the same group will exhibit similar physical and chemical properties. Therefore, potassium is the most similar element to sodium.

NR 2   2111

Ionic compounds are pure substances formed as a result of the attraction between charged particles called ions. A positive metal ion reacts with a negative non-metal ion. Because charged particles are involved, ionic compounds are good electrical conductors. Molecular compounds are pure substances formed when two non-metallic elements combine. Molecular compounds tend to be insulators with low melting and boiling points.

1. *Explain the law of conservation of mass as applied to chemical reactions. Include an example in your response.*

Matter is neither created nor destroyed. It is only changed. The total mass of the products must equal the total mass of the reactants.

For example, 22.3 g of iron reacts with 14.2 g of sulfur to produce 36.5 g of iron sulfide.

Fe + S   →   FeS
22.3 g 14.2 g   36.5 g

2. *What is the difference between the halogen grouping of elements and the noble gas grouping of elements?*

Halogens are the most reactive non-metals listed in the periodic table. They include the elements fluorine, chlorine, bromine, and iodine. These elements are located in the second-last family (group 17). The noble gases are the most stable and non-reactive elements. They include helium, neon, argon, krypton, xenon, and radon. These elements appear on the last grouping (number 18).

3. *Compare Thompson's and Rutherford's contributions to knowledge about the structure of the atom.*

Thompson is credited with discovering the subatomic electron. Rutherford discovered the presence of a nucleus in an atom.

Environmental Chemistry

ENVIRONMENTAL CHEMISTRY

Table of Correlations			
Specific Expectation	**Practice Questions**	**Unit Test Questions**	**2006 PAT**
Students will:			
C.1. Investigate and describe, in general terms, the role of different substances in the environment in supporting or harming humans and other living things.			
C.1.1 identify common organic and inorganic substances that are essential to the health and growth of humans and other living things, and illustrate the roles served by these substances	1, 3, 4	1	
C.1.2 describe in general terms, the forms of organic matter synthesized by plants and animals, including carbohydrates, proteins and lipids	5, 6, 7		
C.1.3 describe and illustrate processes by which chemicals are introduced to the environment or their concentrations are changed	8, 9, 10	2, 4	22
C.1.4 describe the uptake of materials by living things through ingestion or absorption, and investigate and describe evidence that some materials are difficult for organisms to break down or eliminate	11, 12, 13, 14, 34	WR1, 14	
C.1.5 identify questions that may need to be addressed in deciding what substances—in what amounts—can be safely released into the environment	14, 15		
C.2. Identify processes for measuring the quantity of different substances in the environment and for monitoring air and water quality.			
C.2.1 identify substrates and nutrient sources for living things within a variety of environments	17	11	27
C.2.2 describe and illustrate the use of biological monitoring as one method for determining environmental quality	18	12	
C.2.3 identify chemical factors in an environment that might affect the health and distribution of living things in that environment	16, 19, 21	6, NR1	25
C.2.4 apply and interpret measures of chemical concentrations in parts per million, billion or trillion	20, 21, 22	8	28, 29
C.2.5 identify acids, bases, and neutral substances, based on measures of their pH	NR1, 23, 24	10, 13	23
C.2.6 investigate, safely, and describe the effects of acids and bases on each other and on other substances	25, 26		26
C.2.7 describe effects of acids and bases on living things	27		

C.3.	Analyze and evaluate mechanisms affecting the distribution of potentially harmful substances within an environment.			
C.3.1 describe mechanisms for the transfer of materials through air, water and soil; and identify factors that may accelerate or retard distribution	28, 29, 30	7, 9	
C.3.2 describe mechanisms for biodegradation, and interpret information on the biodegradability of different materials	2, 31, 32		24
C.3.3 comprehend information on the biological impacts of hazardous chemicals on local and global environments, by: • interpreting evidence for environmental changes in the vicinity of a substance release • interpreting LD50 data and other information on toxicity • identifying concerns with the disposal of domestic wastes, such as paints and oils, and industrial wastes	33, 36	3, 14	
C.3.4 describe and evaluate methods used to transport, store, and dispose of hazardous household chemicals	37	5	
C.3.5 investigate and evaluate potential risks resulting from consumer practices and industrial processes, and identify processes used in providing information and setting standards to manage these risks	35	NR2	30
C.3.6 identify and evaluate information and evidence related to an issue in which environmental chemistry plays a major role	NR2	WR2	

ENVIRONMENTAL CHEMISTRY

C.1.1   identify common organic and inorganic substances that are essential to the health and growth of humans and other living things, and illustrate the roles served by these substances

COMMON ORGANIC AND INORGANIC SUBSTANCES

All matter is classified as either inorganic or organic in composition. Inorganic matter includes substances that have elements such as magnesium, phosphorus, potassium, and calcium in their molecular structure. These elements are essential for the proper growth of plants and animals for the following reasons:

- Magnesium is essential for carrying out photosynthesis and maintaining metabolic reactions in animals.

- Potassium stimulates protein production in plants and muscle contractions in animals.

- Calcium and phosphorus are essential for carrying out cell division in plants and for growing teeth and bone in animals.

- Nitrogen is required for building proteins. Nitrogen fixing bacteria are found in the roots of some plants that help convert nitrogen into a useable form for the plants.

Organic matter includes the majority of compounds that have the element carbon in their molecular structure. Some of these compounds are essential for proper growth and development. Common organic compounds used by plants and animals are carbohydrates, lipids, and proteins.

Living organisms require inorganic and organic nutrients in varying amounts. Compounds required in large amounts such as, carbohydrates, lipids and oxygen are called macronutrients. Compounds required in much smaller amounts such as vitamin A and iodine are called micronutrients.

Plants and animals require nutrients in specific amounts; too much or too little can be harmful. For example, if soil contains a high level of potassium and a low level of magnesium, the leaves on a plant growing in the soil will develop yellow stripes.

Practice Questions: 1, 3, 4

C.1.2   describe in general terms, the forms of organic matter synthesized by plants and animals, including carbohydrates, proteins and lipids

ORGANIC SUBSTANCES SYNTHESIZED BY PLANTS AND ANIMALS

The organic substances synthesized by plants and animals are carbohydrates, lipids, proteins, and nucleic acids.

Carbohydrates are organic substances made up of carbon, hydrogen, and oxygen atoms. They can be simple molecules, such as glucose, fructose, and sucrose; or complex molecules, such as starch, cellulose, and glycogen. Green plants synthesize glucose during photosynthesis.

Lipids are also composed of carbon, hydrogen, and oxygen atoms. They are fats, oils, and waxes produced by plants and animals. Humans store energy from food in the form of fat, and human skin produces oils for protection. Plants produce oils and fats in their nuts and seeds, such as peanuts, walnuts, and canola seeds. Fat molecules are made up of fatty acids and glycerol.

Proteins are molecules composed of carbon, hydrogen, oxygen, and nitrogen atoms. Proteins are essential for the growth and repair of tissue, and they can be a source of energy. Proteins are made up of **amino acid** molecules joined together and arranged in a specific sequence.

Nucleic acids are the largest complex molecules found in living organisms. A cell contains deoxyribonucleic acid (**DNA**) and ribonucleic acid (**RNA**). A complex molecule of DNA or RNA is composed of phosphate, a simple sugar (ribose or deoxyribose), and nitrogen-containing bases. Nucleic acids are responsible for the transmission of characteristics and for controlling cell activity.

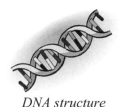

DNA structure

Practice Questions: 5, 6, 7

C.1.3   describe and illustrate processes by which chemicals are introduced to the environment or their concentrations are changed

CHEMICALS INTRODUCED INTO THE ENVIRONMENT

Both natural processes and human activities release chemicals into the environment. Carbon dioxide is released naturally into the air during cellular respiration by animals. Cellular respiration, the process by which your body uses the oxygen and chemicals in food to produce energy, releases carbon dioxide as a by-product. Carbon dioxide and other compounds are also released in the air as a result of human activities, such as driving a car or burning coal to produce electricity. The accumulation of unwanted waste matter in the environment is called **pollution**. Pollution causes changes in the environment that are harmful to living things.

The following activities pollute the environment:

• Solid waste disposal

• Waste water disposal

• Combustion

• Agricultural activities

• Industrial processes

Many of the chemicals introduced into the environment by these processes can be broken down naturally, but some of them cannot. The chemicals that cannot break down accumulate in the environment and have long-term effects on the ecosystem.

AGRICULTURAL ACTIVITIES USE CHEMICALS

Agricultural activities are responsible for introducing many chemicals into the environment. In order to enrich the soil and improve crop yields, farmers use **fertilizer**. Fertilizers contain nitrogen, phosphorus, potassium, and sulfur. These elements are important for plant growth. However, their overuse pollutes soil and water. Fertilizers that leach from the soil into water systems promote excessive plant growth. The decay of these plants results in oxygen depletion.

Farmers also use **pesticides** to improve their crop yields. Pesticides are chemicals designed to kill organisms that damage crops. **Herbicides** are used to kill or control weeds, **insecticides** kill or control insects, and **fungicides** kill fungi. All of these chemicals pose a serious threat to the ecosystem.

SOLID WASTE DISPOSAL

Solid waste is garbage collected from households, industries, and construction sites. While some of this waste can be reused or recycled, a large amount is deposited in landfills. Plastic liners and clay are used in sanitary landfills to prevent chemicals from leaching into the ground.

Some waste is too hazardous to be dumped in a landfill, and this waste is often burned in incinerators. Incinerating garbage produces air pollution.

WASTEWATER DISPOSAL

The wastewater collected from bathrooms, kitchens, and laundry rooms is called **sewage**. Sewage is made up of both dissolved and undissolved substances. In rural areas, septic tanks are used to collect sewage. Bacteria in the septic tank break down the harmful substances before the substances are released into the soil. In urban areas, sewage is pumped to sewage treatment plants. Once the sewage has been broken down by bacteria or other chemical processes, the treated wastewater (called effluent) is released into nearby rivers and lakes.

COMBUSTION

Fossil fuels such as coal, petroleum, and natural gas are often burned in order to release energy. During a combustion reaction with these fuels, large amounts of carbon dioxide and varying amounts of sulfur dioxide are produced. Many combustion particulates are heavier than air, ending up in the soil and water. Sulfur dioxide that is released combines with water in the atmosphere and causes acid rain or snow.

Combustion in vehicles is a major source of ground level ozone. High concentrations of ground level ozone cause breathing problems for people with respiratory diseases.

INDUSTRIAL PROCESSES

Harmful wastes are released into the environment during various industrial processes, such as the processing of crude oil. Crude oil is a mixture of many compounds including those with high toxicity. It is important to minimize the release of these compounds into the air when producing petroleum.

Practice Questions: 8, 9, 10

C.1.4   describe the uptake of materials by living things through ingestion or absorption, and investigate and describe evidence that some materials are difficult for organisms to break down or eliminate

ABSORPTION OF NUTRIENTS IN PLANTS

Both organic and inorganic chemical compounds are absorbed by plants. Plants absorb these substances from the air and from the soil. Water is required to transport nutrients to the cells and to carry waste products out of the cells. In plants, osmosis is one of the processes by which water in the soil moves into the root cells of a plant. The water passes through a semi-permeable membrane, the cell wall, from an area that has a high concentration of water to an area of low concentration of water. In the diagram the water in side A will move into side B through osmosis even though there is more sugar, and therefore less water, in side A. This is the opposite of diffusion where compounds move from areas of higher concentration to areas of lower concentration.

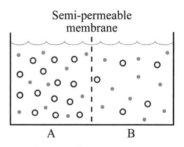

Semi-permeable membrane

A   B

o - Sugar molecule
• - Water molecule

Plants need to absorb nutrients through their roots. The concentrations of these nutrients can be higher in the roots than in the surrounding soil. This means that the nutrients needed in high concentrations will not diffuse into plant roots from the soil. The roots absorb high amounts of these nutrients through a process called active transport. Active transport is the movement of material from an area of low concentration to an area of high concentration. Unlike osmosis and diffusion, this process requires energy.

INGESTION AND ABSORPTION OF NUTRIENTS IN ANIMALS

Humans and other animals get nutrients from the food they eat. The process of taking in food is called **ingestion**. The food is broken down mechanically and chemically into simpler substances that can be used by the body. **Hydrolysis** is a process in which large organic molecules, such as sugars, are broken down with water. Complex maltose sugars are hydrolyzed into simple glucose sugars. Once the maltose sugar has been broken down, the glucose nutrients are small enough to be absorbed into the blood stream. The blood transports the nutrients to appropriate blood cells for use or storage.

BIOACCUMULATION AND BIOMAGNIFICATION

When harmful chemicals are introduced into an environment, they can be absorbed by living organisms. Some toxic chemical compounds that are absorbed into an organism's body do not easily break down and do not get removed from the organism's body. Even if there are very low levels of the toxic compound in an organism's environment, the compound can accumulate in the organism's body over time, making the organism sick or even killing it. The process of low levels of chemicals building up in the bodies of living organisms is called **bioaccumulation**.

Each level of the food chain is called a trophic level. Producers make up the first trophic level, primary consumers (herbivores) make up the second trophic level, and secondary consumers (carnivores) make up the tertiary (third) and higher trophic levels. Bioaccumulation can affect organisms at each trophic level.

Because toxic substances that bioaccumulate become part of the tissues of an organism's body, they will be passed on when that organism is eaten. As these compounds are passed up through each trophic level, they accumulate in greater concentrations in organisms of higher trophic levels. This process is called **biomagnification**.

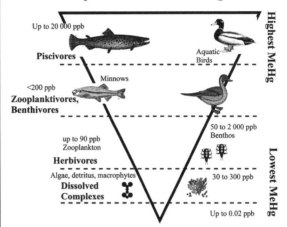

The given diagram shows a food pyramid with trophic levels and relative concentrations of harmful substances (in ppm) at each level.

The effect of a "red tide" is an example of how bioaccumulation affects consumers at different trophic levels. A harmful algal bloom or "red tide" occurs in the ocean when there is the rapid reproduction of single-celled algae, or phytoplankton, which produces a natural toxin. When toxin-producing phytoplankton begin to reproduce rapidly, the organisms that feed on them accumulate the toxin in their bodies. Shellfish are filter-feeders that store the toxins from "red tides" in their bodies for several weeks. Shellfish are at the second trophic level and are not usually severely harmed by the toxin but these harmful algal blooms can make organisms at higher trophic levels that eat the shellfish such as fish, whales, sea lions, and people very ill.

Practice Questions: 11, 12, 13, 14, 34

C.1.5   *identify questions that may need to be addressed in deciding what substances— in what amounts—can be safely released into the environment*

SAFE RELEASE OF SUBSTANCES INTO THE ENVIRONMENT

Motor vehicles are a primary source of air pollution. Combustion in the engine of a motor vehicle releases nitrogen oxide, carbon monoxide, and carbon dioxide pollutants into the air. What level of pollution emissions by vehicles is considered to be acceptable? How can vehicle emissions be reduced to safe levels? These are some of the questions that need to be addressed.

In an attempt to reduce the pollution emissions from motor vehicles, car manufacturers have designed more energy efficient engines that burn less fuel. Car makers have also designed a catalytic converter for the muffler system that removes pollutants from the vehicle exhaust. Human actions like driving small vehicles, carpooling, and taking public transit help to reduce emissions in the atmosphere.

Landfills are specially designed areas where solid wastes are disposed of. Selecting a landfill site is not an easy task. The location must be one that is economical to get to, environmentally safe, and large enough to store the increasing amount of household waste. Landfills are constructed with a thick clay liner which prevents the garbage leachate from seeping into the nearby water system. Methane gas produced by the rotting garbage in a landfill must be safely contained. Sometimes the gas is collected and piped to a power plant where it is used as fuel to produce electricity.

Finding a suitable landfill site is becoming more difficult. That is why it is important to reduce the waste matter that ends up in a landfill. Personal actions such as reusing and recycling can reduce the amount of solid waste taken to landfills.

It is important to consider the effects that natural and human activities have on the environment and to take steps to reduce the impact of these processes.

Practice Questions: 14, 15

C.2.1   *identify substrates and nutrient sources for living things within a variety of environments*

SUBSTRATE AND NUTRIENT SOURCES

A **substrate** is any surface on which a plant or animal lives or moves. It may be abiotic or biotic. In biological terms, nutrient stores contained in the substrate are essential to the survival of organisms.

Coral reefs are made up of millions of animals called polyps that secrete calcium carbonate shells. These hard shells are the substrate, or living area, for molluscs, worms, crustaceans, echinoderms (such as sea cucumbers and sea urchins), and sponges. Food particles that settle on the surface of the coral provide nutrients to feed the organisms that are living there. Algae use the reef as a substrate, while organisms such as the sea urchin use the algae as food.

The forest floor is one of the richest sources of nutrients in a forest ecosystem. It is mainly made up of decaying vegetation such as branches and leaves. As they decay, minerals and organic compounds are released and added to the nutrient-rich soil. The soil provides the substrate for a large number of decomposers such as bacteria, fungi, algae, and worms, as well as for the trees and other vegetation.

Practice Question: 17

C.2.2 describe and illustrate the use of biological monitoring as one method for determining environmental quality

BIOLOGICAL MONITORING

The invertebrate aquatic organisms found in a water habitat are an excellent indicator of water quality.

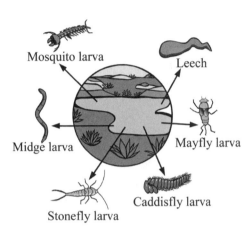

Mosquito larva
Leech
Midge larva
Mayfly larva
Stonefly larva
Caddisfly larva

Factors such as temperature, pH, and dissolved oxygen affect the kind of organisms found in water habitats. Organisms living in a stagnant pond are different from the organisms living in a stream or large lake.

Biological Indicators of Dissolved Oxygen in Water		
Poor Quality (0 to 4 parts per million of oxygen)	Moderate Quality (5 to 8 parts per million of oxygen)	Good Quality (9 to 10 parts per million of oxygen)
Midge larvae Leech Mosquito Wriggler	Freshwater clam Dragonfly nymph Fairy shrimp	Caddisfly larvae Stonefly larvae Mayfly larvae

If a water supply has lots of midge larvae, some leeches, and no caddisfly larvae, it has little dissolved oxygen and is poor quality. If the water has caddisfly and mayfly larvae, it is rich in dissolved oxygen and is good quality.

THE IMPORTANCE OF MONITORING AIR QUALITY

Air is a blend of several gases. It is just as important as water for sustaining life.

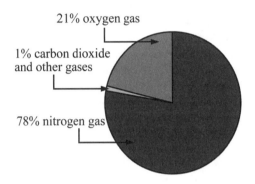

21% oxygen gas
1% carbon dioxide and other gases
78% nitrogen gas

The quality of air should be carefully monitored and good air quality maintained. Collecting data about chemicals in the air provides information about immediate and long-term trends. Presently there is concern about emissions of sulfur dioxide, nitrogen oxide, carbon dioxide, and chlorofluorocarbons in the atmosphere and the effect of these emissions on the environment.

Practice Question: 18

C.2.3 identify chemical factors in an environment that might affect the health and distribution of living things in that environment

CHEMICAL FACTORS AFFECTING THE DISTRIBUTION OF LIVING THINGS

Chemical concentrations indicate the quality of water and may affect the distribution of living organisms within an ecosystem.

Water has oxygen dissolved within it, which is essential for the survival of aquatic life. The amount of oxygen dissolved in water depends on factors such as the temperature, the rate of photosynthesis, and the number of organisms present in that water. The number and diversity of living things is greater in water that has a good supply of dissolved oxygen.

Phosphates and nitrates enter the water supply through sewage and runoff containing fertilizers. Phosphorus and nitrogen are elements essential for living organisms, but high concentrations of these elements can cause adverse effects in an ecosystem. These chemicals cause an overgrowth of algae in the aquatic system.

Bacteria break down dead plant matter and use oxygen in the process. This depletes the supply of oxygen for plants and animals living in the water.

Natural rainwater has an average pH of 5 and a typical range from pH 4.5 to 5.6. However, any precipitation with a pH lower than 5.6 is called **acid rain**. When acid rain reaches the ground, it mixes with other water sources, increasing the acidity of these water sources. Fewer organisms are able to survive in an acidic environment.

Pesticides are chemicals that farmers use to control unwanted insects and rodents. Pesticides usually have long term effects because they remain in the environment long after their intended use. It is possible that insects can develop a tolerance to a certain pesticide, creating the need for a stronger pesticide. Chemical pesticides can make the water and soil toxic. As well, some pesticides are not broken down within organisms and can bioaccumulate.

Elements such as mercury, copper, lead, zinc, cadmium, and nickel are **heavy metals**. These elements are used in many commercial products such as batteries, thermometers, and electronic equipment. Heavy metals can enter the water system and accumulate in the bodies of animals. This causes illness, deformities, and death.

Practice Questions: 16, 19, 21

C.2.4 apply and interpret measures of chemical concentrations in parts per million, billion or trillion

MEASURING IN PARTS PER MILLION

Concentrations of chemicals in the environment are commonly measured in parts per million (ppm) or milligrams per litre (mg/L).

$$\text{ppm} = \frac{\text{grams of solute}}{\text{grams of solution}} \times 10^6$$

$$\frac{\text{mg}}{\text{litre}} = \frac{\text{milligram of solute}}{\text{litre of solution}}$$

Example

One part per million means one unit of chemical is found in one million units of solution. If 1 mL of food colouring is dissolved in 999 mL of water, what is the concentration of the food colouring in the water in ppm?

Solution

Let x be ppm.
999 mL water + 1 mL food colouring = 1 000 mL

$$\frac{1 \text{ mL}}{1\ 000 \text{ mL}} = \frac{x}{1\ 000\ 000}$$
$$x = 1\ 000 \text{ ppm}$$

The concentration of food colouring is 1 000 ppm.

Practice Questions: 20, 21, 22

C.2.5 identify acids, bases, and neutral substances based on measures of their pH

ACIDS, BASES, AND NEUTRAL SUBSTANCES

An **acid** is a compound that, when dissolved in water, has a pH less than 7. An acidic solution that has a pH of 1 would be a much stronger acid than a solution with a pH of 4. Stomach acid (pH 1) is more acidic than tomato juice (pH 4). Lemon juice is another example of an acid.

A **base** is a compound that forms a solution with a pH higher than 7. A solution with a pH of 14 is a strong base. Bases taste bitter and feel slippery. Baking soda is an example of a base. **Neutral substances** are neither acidic nor basic and have a pH of 7. Distilled water and blood are neutral substances.

The acidity of a solution is described by **pH**. The pH is a measure of the concentration of the hydrogen ions present in that solution. Substances have pH levels between 0 and 14 on the pH scale.

The difference between one whole number and the next on the pH scale represents a ten-fold difference in the concentration of hydrogen. For example, a substance with a pH of 2 is 10 times more acidic than a substance with a pH of 3 and 100 times more acidic than a substance with a pH of 4 ($10 \times 10 = 100$).

To identify a substance as an acid, a base, or neutral, use a chemical indicator such as pH paper. For example, red litmus paper turns blue in a base and remains unaffected in an acid. Blue litmus paper turns red in an acid and remains unaffected in a base. Other chemical indicators are phenolphthalein and bromothymol blue.

Practice Questions: NR1, 23, 24

C.2.6 investigate, safely, and describe the effects of acids and bases on each other and on other substances

NEUTRALIZATION

A **neutralization** reaction is a reaction between an acid and a base. When an acid reacts with a base, salt and water are produced.

Example

$$HCl_{(aq)} \quad + \quad NaOH_{(aq)} \rightarrow \quad NaCl_{(s)} \quad + \quad H_2O_{(l)}$$

| Hydrochloric acid (an acid) | Sodium hydroxide (a base) | Sodium chloride (salt) | Water |

Practice Questions: 25, 26

C.2.7 describe effects of acids and bases on living things

EFFECTS OF ACIDS AND BASES ON ORGANISMS

Most industrial processes emit waste gases such as carbon dioxide, sulfur dioxide, and nitrogen oxide. These gases dissolve in water droplets in the air to form acids.  Carbon dioxide forms carbonic acid, sulfur dioxide forms sulfuric acid, and nitrogen oxide forms nitric acid. Acid rain pollution occurs when the water droplets containing these dissolved gases fall to the ground and run into lakes and ponds. Acid rain also causes chemical changes in the soil, reducing its fertility. Acid rain hinders the growth of some plants, corrodes metal surfaces, and deteriorates limestone and marble.

The effects of acid rain can be reduced by treating lakes with lime (calcium oxide). Lime is dissolved into the water and neutralizes the acid present in the lake water.

Practice Question: 27

C.3.1 describe mechanisms for the transfer of materials through air, water and soil; and identify factors that may accelerate or retard distribution

TRANSPORT OF MATERIAL THROUGH AIR, SOIL, AND WATER

The transport of substances in the environment occurs in three stages: the **release** of chemicals from the source, the **dispersion** of chemicals into the atmosphere, and the **deposition** of chemicals in soil or water.

Pollutants transported through air are called airborne pollutants. The direction and distance travelled by airborne chemicals is determined by factors such as the properties of the chemical pollutants, the speed of the wind, and the direction of the wind.

Hazardous chemicals can enter into surface water as effluent from sewage treatment plants or runoff from agricultural fields that use pesticides and fertilizers. If a low concentration of a chemical can be dissolved in water and dispersed over a wide area, the toxicity of the chemical will be reduced. The problem lies with insoluble substances deposited near the pollution source. As they accumulate, the substances will create an area of contamination.

Water flows through the ground and seeps down in the soil. It will eventually reach the groundwater zone. Groundwater moves, but the rate at which it moves is very slow.

This means that it takes a long time for pollutants dissolved in groundwater to disperse. If the groundwater is used as drinking water, the toxic pollutants can become a health hazard.

The movement of groundwater is affected by pores in the soil. Permeable soil has larger pores and more space between particles. It is easier for pollutants to flow and spread through permeable soil.

Soil pollution by hydrocarbons takes place as a result of the use of fossil fuels in vehicles and industries. These hydrocarbons do not dissolve in water; they cling to the soil particles, changing the soil properties. Most hydrocarbons are toxic to both plants and animals.

Practice Questions: 28, 29, 30

C.3.2 describe mechanisms for biodegradation, and interpret information on the biodegradability of different materials

BIODEGRADATION

The concentration of pollutants in the environment can be decreased naturally. Certain organisms, such as bacteria, fungi and earthworms, can decompose pollutants in the soil. These organisms break down complex organic molecules into simpler substances in a process called **biodegradation**. Bacteria are especially important in this process. Some bacteria require oxygen to carry out biodegradation. When this process needs oxygen, the process is referred to as **aerobic biodegradation**.

Other bacteria can only survive under conditions with no oxygen. These bacteria decompose organic material in **anaerobic biodegradation.**

The process of biodegradation is affected by the availability of nutrients, pH, temperature, soil moisture, and oxygen supply. An environment that is too cold or too dry is unfavourable for microorganisms to decompose matter.

Bioreactors have been built to increase the rate of biodegradation. Bioreactors are designed to provide the optimal conditions for biodegradation at all times. A sewage treatment plant has bioreactors to speed up the decomposition of sewage.

The rate of biodegradation can also be increased by planting vegetation in the area. Bacteria and fungi are more likely to inhabit soil where plants are present.

Practice Questions: 2, 31, 32

C.3.3 *comprehend information on the biological impacts of hazardous chemicals on local and global environments, by:*

- *interpreting evidence for environmental changes in the vicinity of a substance release*
- *interpreting LD50 data and other information on toxicity*
- *identifying concerns with the disposal of domestic wastes, such as paints and oils, and industrial wastes*

IMPACTS OF HAZARDOUS CHEMICALS

It is important to properly dispose of hazardous chemicals. Even a small amount of a chemical released into the environment can have detrimental effects. The harmful effects of a toxin or hazardous chemical often increase through biomagnification as it moves through the food chain. For example, if a small quantity of mercury leaked into a lake, it would be absorbed by phytoplankton. Small fish that feed on the phytoplankton might absorb some toxins from the water, but they would also take in all the mercury that the phytoplankton had absorbed. Since one fish would eat many phytoplankton, the mercury concentration would be many times higher in the fish than in the phytoplankton. The mercury level would be magnified again when larger fish eat the smaller fish. An osprey that then eats the larger fish would have the highest concentration of mercury.

Certain chemical substances, such as household cleaners, fertilizers, pesticides, paints, and automotive fuels, are hazardous to your health. If not handled properly, they can be toxic.

The use of pesticides and the combination of pesticides can produce poisoning effects. This is referred to as the chemical's **toxicity**. Toxicity describes how poisonous a substance is.

To compare the toxicity of certain chemicals, scientists use a measurement called the **median lethal dose** or LD_{50}. The LD_{50} is the dose of a toxic substance required to kill half the members of a tested population after a specified test duration.

For example, the LD_{50} dosage of DDT in rats is 87 mg/kg. Half the rats in a population would die if given a dosage of 87 mg/kg of DDT.

Practice Questions: 33, 36

C.3.4 *describe and evaluate methods used to transport, store, and dispose of hazardous household chemicals*

C.3.5 *investigate and evaluate potential risks resulting from consumer practices and industrial processes, and identify processes used in providing information and setting standards to manage these risks*

TRANSPORT, STORAGE, AND DISPOSAL OF HAZARDOUS CHEMICALS

Students working in laboratories must be familiar with the Workplace Hazardous Material Information System (**WHMIS**). WHMIS labels on containers specify the type of hazardous chemicals in the containers. The barrels in the illustration contain flammable chemicals.

Material Safety Data Sheets (**MSDS**) give detailed descriptions of chemical products. An MSDS contains information about the composition, physical properties, and chemical features of the chemical product. It describes the precautions to be taken while handling, storing, transporting, or disposing of that product.

Chemicals are not just found in a laboratory. Many chemicals are found at home. Cleaners, fertilizers, pesticides, paints, and automotive fuels are hazardous to human health and they can be toxic if not handled properly.

When storing hazardous chemicals, be sure to take the following precautions:

- Leave products in their original containers with their labels intact.

- Keep the chemicals out of the reach of children.

- Keep containers tightly closed with a lid.

- Store chemicals in a cool, dry place.

- Do not store flammable liquids in glass containers.

- Store corrosive, flammable, reactive, and poisonous chemicals separately.

- Keep oxidizers (such as hydrogen peroxide, $H_2O_{2(l)}$) away from flammable chemicals.

- Return chemicals to their proper locations after use.

- Safely discard hazardous chemicals if they have expired.

Hazardous chemicals should not be poured down the drain, into sewers, into septic systems, or into the soil. Do not throw chemicals in the garbage. There are hazardous waste collection sites where wastes such as oil, paints, and household cleaners can be disposed of. It is very important to transport, store, and dispose of hazardous chemicals properly.

Practice Questions: 35, 37

C.3.6 *identify and evaluate information and evidence related to an issue in which environmental chemistry plays a major role*

ENVIRONMENTAL CHEMISTRY

Environmental chemistry is the study of the chemical processes in an environment.. Environmental chemists study which chemicals are present naturally in an ecosystem, their concentrations, and their effects on the natural environment. Understanding environmental chemistry is an important first step towards understanding how a clean environment works and how pollutants change things.

Environmental chemistry is used by Environment Canada and environmental research bodies around the world in order to identify the source of pollutants and their potential polluting impacts on the environment.

Practice Question: NR2

PRACTICE QUESTIONS—ENVIRONMENTAL CHEMISTRY

Use the following information to answer the next question.

Inorganic minerals are necessary for the growth of the human body.

1. Which two inorganic elements are found in the composition of bones and teeth?
   A. Iron and sulfur
   B. Sulfur and chlorine
   C. Sodium and potassium
   D. Calcium and phosphorus

2. In most sewage treatment processes, there is a stage at which the waste is broken down by bacteria. The fact that this waste can be broken down by bacteria indicates that the waste is
   A. biodegradable
   B. organic
   C. nontoxic
   D. natural

3. Certain types of bacteria present in the roots of legume plants are responsible for
   A. nitrogen fixation
   B. cleaning up the soil
   C. decomposing dead matter
   D. replenishing phosphorus in the soil

Use the following information to answer the next question.

In order to carry out certain life activities efficiently, living organisms need some nutrients in small quantities (micronutrients) and other nutrients in relatively large amounts (macronutrients).

4. Which of the following elements is **not** a macronutrient?
   A. Calcium
   B. Fluorine
   C. Nitrogen
   D. Phosphorus

5. The most abundant food type that plants provide for human consumption is
   A. carbohydrates
   B. proteins
   C. oils
   D. fats

6. Which of the following organic compounds found in living organisms are responsible for heredity?
   A. Fats
   B. Proteins
   C. Nucleic acids
   D. Carbohydrates

7. The organic substances containing carbon, hydrogen, and nitrogen that are responsible for the growth and repair of worn-out tissues are
   A. carbohydrates
   B. nucleic acids
   C. proteins
   D. lipids

8. Which of the following substances is **not** a gaseous air pollutant?

   A. Nitrogen oxide

   B. Hydrogen sulfide

   C. Sulfur dioxide

   D. Carbon

9. Wastewater from kitchens, bathrooms, and laundries is treated in sewage treatment plants. The treated water is called

   A. household wastewater

   B. disinfected water

   C. effluent

   D. sewage

10. Solid hazardous wastes are destroyed in

    A. septic tanks

    B. incinerators

    C. sanitary landfills

    D. sewage treatment plants

11. The process that uses energy to move nutrients from an area of low concentration to an area of high concentration is called

    A. osmosis

    B. diffusion

    C. capillary action

    D. active transport

Use the following information to answer the next question.

The chemical breakdown of starch into sugar occurs in the mouth. This reaction uses water present in the saliva.

12. A chemical reaction that requires water to break down large molecules into smaller molecules is called

    A. ingestion

    B. oxidation

    C. hydrolysis

    D. electrolysis

13. Roots of plants absorb water from the soil through the process of

    A. passive transport

    B. active transport

    C. absorption

    D. osmosis

14. The pesticide DDT was used in the 1940's to control mosquito levels and reduce malaria. While it was effective as an insecticide it also contaminated lakes and streams and ended up in the food chain. Which of the following statements about DDT is most likely **false**?

    A. DDT levels increased in fish through bioaccumulation

    B. DDT levels increased in fish eating falcons through biomagnification

    C. DDT levels increased in lake weeds through biomagnification.

    D. DDT levels increased in fish eating falcons through bioaccumulation

The construction of a new fertilizer plant has
been approved of for Rapid City, but many
citizens are worried about environmental issues
that could arise. Citizens were asked to provide
questions to the mayor about their concerns.

Questions Asked by the Citizens

1. How will the plant affect the smell of
   the air?

2. Will the chemicals be diluted before being
   released into the environment?

3. Will either the products or by-products stay
   in the environment?

4. Will the construction of the plant improve
   the local economy?

15. The questions related to environmental issues
    are indicated by the numbers
    A. 1, 2, and 4
    B. 1, 2, and 3
    C. 1, 3, and 4
    D. 2, 3, and 4

16. Occasionally, raw sewage is dumped directly
    into a lake or river. The major effect that this
    has on the water environment is that the
    A. oxygen content of the water drops
    B. aquatic plant growth decreases
    C. water becomes poisoned
    D. bacteria die

17. Lichens are organisms that can be found even
    in the Arctic and on the highest mountains.
    The substrate on which lichens grow is
    A. rock
    B. snow
    C. water
    D. polyps

18. Which of the following biological indicators is
    least likely to be used to determine the quality
    of water in a lake?
    A. Leeches
    B. Ducks
    C. Frogs
    D. Fish

19. Acid rain is any precipitation that has a pH
    lower than
    A. 4.9
    B. 5.2
    C. 5.6
    D. 7.2

The oxygen content of
the atmosphere is
approximately 21%, and
the oxygen concentration
of typical lake water is
about 0.001%.

20. Which of the following rows identifies the
    concentrations of oxygen in the atmosphere
    and lake water in ppm?

Row	Oxygen in Atmosphere (ppm)	Oxygen in Lake Water (ppm)
A.	210 000	10
B.	21	0.001
C.	21 000 000	1 000
D.	21×10^6	1×10^3

Use the following information to answer the next question.

Before investigating animal life in a pond, you refer to your field manual and find the following information.

Oxygen Requirements of Some Freshwater Invertebrates

OXYGEN CONCENTRATION (mg/L)	ORGANISMS PRESENT
8 and above (excellent level)	• large variety of invertebrates (insect larvae of many kinds, worms, etc)
6 (good level)	• a few mayfly larvae • some stonefly larvae • many midge larvae • many worms, including leeches
4 (critical level)	• many midge larvae • many worms, including leeches
2 (low level)	• many midge larvae • some worms, including leeches
less than 2 (very low level)	• some midge larvae • some worms

21. You collect water samples from the pond and find more midge larvae than mayfly larvae. You infer that the oxygen concentration in this pond is **most likely**.

    A. 6 mg/L

    B. 4 mg/L

    C. 2 mg/L

    D. less than 2 mg/L

Source: PAT, 1999

22. A solution was made by dissolving 3 mL of food colouring in 997 mL of water. In this solution, the concentration of food colouring is

    A. 18 ppm

    B. 300 ppm

    C. 1 800 ppm

    D. 3 000 ppm

23. On the pH scale, neutral is indicated by the number

    A. 0

    B. 1

    C. 5

    D. 7

Use the following information to answer the next question.

Properties

1. Tastes sour

2. Tastes bitter

3. Does not dissolve in water

4. Dissolves in water

5. pH less than 7

6. pH greater than 7

7. Turns litmus paper blue

8. Turns litmus paper red

Numerical Response

1. The properties of acids given in the chart, listed in ascending numerical order, are ____, ____, ____, ____. (Record your answer as a **four-digit** number.)

Use the following information to answer the next question.

To study the effects of the campsite on the soil, you collected soil samples from four different sites in the camp area before the camp was set up, during the project, and after the campsite was removed. This chart shows the data you collected.

	pH Level		
Site	**Before**	**During**	**After**
1	7.6	7.2	6.6
2	7.8	7.5	6.9
3	7.5	7.4	7.4
4	7.4	6.9	6.5

24. You conclude that the activities at the campsite caused the soil to become

   A. neutral

   B. more basic

   C. more acidic

   D. polluted

Source: PAT, 1999

Use the following information to answer the next question.

A scientist wanted to know which one of three cities received the most acidic rain. The scientist conducted the following experiment.

I. A 50 mL sample of rain from each city was carefully measured.

II. A base was added to each sample, one drop at a time.

III. The number of drops of base required to bring each sample to pH 7 was counted.

25. What type of reaction did the scientist perform to test for acidity?

   A. Oxidation

   B. Reduction

   C. Equalization

   D. Neutralization

Use the following information to answer the next question.

Frank was testing a sample of an unknown acidic liquid in science class. Frank accidentally spilled some of the liquid on his hand.

26. The first thing Frank should do after spilling the liquid is

   A. put a neutralizing agent on his hand

   B. dry his hand on his pants

   C. leave his wet hand to air dry

   D. rinse his hand in water

27. Which of the following phenomena is an effect of acid rain?

   A. Global warming

   B. Depletion of ozone layer

   C. Increase in the pH of soil

   D. Decrease in the pH of bodies of water

28. Airborne pollutants are generally transported eastward in Alberta as a result of the

   A. prevailing westerly winds

   B. location of the Rocky Mountains

   C. rotation of Earth in a 24-hour period

   D. small amounts of snowfall and rainfall

29. The tiny spaces between soil particles through which water flows are called

  A. holes

  B. pores

  C. membranes

  D. contaminants

30. Water that soaks through the soil and carries dissolved substances into the soil is called

  A. filtrate

  B. leachate

  C. acid rain

  D. contaminant

31. Which of the following rows provides an example of biodegradable and non-biodegradable material, respectively?

Row	Biodegradable	Non-biodegradable
A.	Wood	Plastic
B.	Metal	Paper
C.	Water	Oil
D.	Styrofoam	Rock

32. Organic waste can be broken down through a process called

  A. biotechnology

  B. biodegradation

  C. bioaccumulation

  D. biomagnification

Use the following information to answer the next question.

Treated waste water from the workers' housing is discharged into a river. A delegate interested in water quality wants to know more about the impact of the waste water on the river system. The tar sands representative shows the delegate the results of a study in which water samples were collected from six different sites along the river.

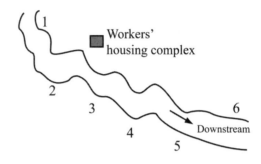

The oxygen concentration for each sample was determined and the following chart was made.

Site Number	Oxygen Concentration (mg/L)
1	12.0
2	12.5
3	8.0
4	3.5
5	2.0
6	5.0

33. Based on this data, the delegate inferred that immediately downstream from the workers' housing the treated waste water discharged

  A. had no effect on the quality of river water

  B. added toxic chemicals to the river water

  C. improved the abiotic conditions of the river water

  D. decreased the concentration of oxygen of the river water

Source: PAT, 1999

34. The increase in the amount of harmful substances at each trophic level of the food chain is called

    A. biomagnification

    B. biodegradation

    C. intensification

    D. concentration

35. Which of the following diagrams represents the WHMIS symbol for compressed gas?

    A.

    B.

    C.

    D.

36. The LD_{50} is the standard used to compare the toxicity of substances. LD_{50} means that

    A. 50 animals would die if they consumed a dose of the toxic substance

    B. 50% of animals would die if they consumed a dose of the toxic substance

    C. 50% of the test population of animals would die if they consumed a specific dose of the toxic substance

    D. 50% of the test population of animals would die if they consumed any amount of the toxic substance

37. An MSDS provides all the following information about a product **except**

    A. the product's composition

    B. methods of use for the product

    C. the product's chemical features

    D. precautions for handling and storing the product

Use the following information to answer the next question.

Many human activities negatively affect water quality. Four human activities are given.

1. A coal-burning factory, which emits sulfur dioxide, is built near a river.

2. A logging company cuts down most of the trees close to a river.

3. Cattle manure is dumped near a river.

4. Raw sewage is accidentally dumped into a river.

Numerical Response

2. Match each of the given human activities with the effect it would have on the river.

    _____   _____   _____   _____

Decrease in oxygen levels	Decrease in pH of the water	Increase in phosphate levels	Increase in sediment in the water

(Record your answer as a **four-digit** number.)

ANSWERS AND SOLUTIONS—PRACTICE QUESTIONS

1. D	9. C	17. A	24. C	32. B
2. A	10. B	18. B	25. D	33. D
3. A	11. D	19. C	26. D	34. A
4. B	12. C	20. A	27. D	35. A
5. A	13. D	21. A	28. A	36. C
6. C	14. C	22. D	29. B	37. B
7. C	15. B	23. D	30. B	NR2. 4132
8. D	16. A	NR1. 1458	31. A	

1. D

Bones and teeth are made up of the salts of calcium and phosphorus. That is why nutritionists suggest drinking milk. Milk contains calcium.

2. A

Biodegradable means that the substance can be broken down or decomposed by microorganisms.

3. A

Certain types of bacteria present in the roots of legume plants are responsible for nitrogen fixation. These bacteria are able to convert atmospheric nitrogen to useful nitrates in the root nodules. The bacteria and the root nodules have a symbiotic association. Both the bacteria and the plants benefit from the relationship.

4. B

Fluorine is not a macronutrient. Nutrients that are required for the growth and development of plants in a considerably high amount are called macronutrients. Examples are nitrogen, phosphorus, and potassium. Only small quantities of fluorine are required, so it is not a macronutrient.

5. A

Human nutrition depends directly or indirectly on plants. Plants carry out a process called photosynthesis. As a result, plants synthesize carbohydrates, which are then consumed as food by living organisms, including humans.

6. C

Nucleic acids include DNA and RNA. These organic compounds are found in the cells of living organisms and are responsible for heredity. Deoxyribonucleic acid and ribonucleic acid are the most complex organic compounds present in the cells of living organisms and are responsible for the transmission of characteristics to the next generation.

7. C

Proteins are organic compounds containing carbon, hydrogen, and nitrogen. Proteins are synthesized in your body. They are responsible for the growth and repair of worn-out tissues.

8. D

Carbon is a solid. It is an element that is part of all living things. However, carbon compounds like carbon monoxide and carbon dioxide are gases that can be air pollutants.

FUN, FRIENDSHIP AND ADVENTURE

Girl greatness starts here.

1910-2010 Girl Greatness Starts Here
Le leadership des filles commence ici

Girl Guides
of Canada
Guides
du Canada

JOIN TODAY!

1-800-565-8111
girlguides.ca

Join the next generation of engineers and change the world.

Protect the environment

Invent clean, sustainable forms of energy

Create new medical technologies and treatments

Discover new ways to use nanotechnology

Fight poverty by developing affordable technology

Are you an engineer?
Visit www.engineering.ualberta.ca

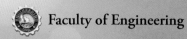

9. **C**

Wastewater is treated in a sewage treatment plant and the treated water is called effluent. Effluent is nearly 99% pure water.

10. **B**

Solid hazardous wastes are destroyed in incinerators. Sanitary landfills, sewage treatment plants, or septic tanks are not able to remove these hazardous wastes.

11. **D**

In active transport, energy is used to move nutrients from an area of low concentration to an area of high concentration. Roots acquire minerals from the soil through active transport.

12. **C**

Hydrolysis is a chemical reaction in which a chemical compound is broken down when water is added. Maltose sugar and water create glucose sugar.

13. **D**

Roots of plants absorb water from the soil through the process of osmosis. Osmosis occurs through a selectively permeable membrane. It is specific to water. Water molecules from the soil diffuse into the cells of roots through the cell membranes of root hairs.

14. **C**

The biomagnification of DDT or other chemicals occurs in higher trophic levels. Lake weeds are in the first trophic level as producers.

15. **B**

The issues relating to the environment are the smell of the air, the release of chemicals into the air, and whether or not the chemicals will remain in the environment.

16. **A**

Raw sewage in the water will be decomposed by bacteria. The decomposition uses oxygen and will deplete the oxygen level in the water.

17. **A**

Lichens grow on rocks, hence their substrate is rocks. Lichens obtain nutrients from this substrate.

18. **B**

A species that is used to monitor the health of a lake ecosystem is called an indicator species. Different aquatic systems can use different organisms to estimate water quality. The most common organisms used are leeches, amphibians, and fish. Birds are rarely used as an indicator species, although in certain aquatic systems, bird populations can reflect changes in water quality.

19. **C**

Any precipitation that has a pH lower than 5.6 is acidic. Various gases such as sulfur dioxide and nitrogen dioxide dissolve in water droplets to make the rainwater acidic.

20. **A**

Compare the % ration to a ppm ratio.

Oxygen in Atmosphere	Oxygen in Lake Water
$\dfrac{21}{100} = \dfrac{x}{1\,000\,000}$ $x = 210\,000$ ppm	$\dfrac{0.001}{100} = \dfrac{x}{1\,000\,000}$ $x = 10$ ppm

21. **A**

The most likely level of oxygen concentration is 6 mg/L or higher. At levels below 6 mg/L, the chart indicates that no mayfly larvae are present.

22. D

The unit ppm means parts per million.
It is calculated as follows:

The total volume of the solution is 1 000mL.
(3 mL food colouring + 997 mL solution
= 1 000 mL)

$$3 \text{ mL}:1\,000 \text{ mL} = x:1\,000\,000$$
$$x = \frac{3 \text{ mL} \times 1\,000\,000}{1\,000 \text{ mL}}$$
$$= 3\,000 \text{ ppm}$$

23. D

On the pH scale, lower than 7 indicates that the substance is acidic and higher than 7 means that it is basic. A neutral substance is neither acidic nor basic and has a pH of 7.

NR 1   1458

Acids taste sour (1), dissolve easily in water (4), have a pH of less than 7 (5), and cause litmus paper to turn red (8).

24. C

The pH scale expresses how acidic or basic a substance is. The lower the pH is, the more acidic the substance. The higher the pH is, the more basic the substance. A drop in pH means that the substance becomes more acidic. There was a drop in pH at every site. The activities must have caused the soil to become more acidic.

25. D

The scientist determined the degree of acidity by neutralizing the acidic water with a base.

26. D

The unknown acidic liquid is potentially hazardous. In order to be completely safe, Frank should dilute the substance to the greatest extent possible. Using a neutralizing agent is not a good idea since the liquid has unknown properties.

27. D

Rain that contains strong acids dissolved in water is called acid rain. The pH of acid rain is low. When acid rain falls into surface bodies of water such as lakes and ponds, it lowers their pH. Global warming is mainly caused by greenhouse gases such as carbon dioxide and water vapour present in the atmosphere. Ozone layer depletion is mainly caused by chlorofluorocarbons (CFCs). Acid rain can lower the pH of soil. Soil can be seriously damaged by acid rain. However, acid rain cannot increase the pH of soil.

28. A

Pollutants are spread through the air by wind currents. In Alberta, the westerly winds are responsible for the eastward movement of pollutants.

29. B

Pores are the tiny spaces between soil particles through which water flows. Ground water seeps through the tiny spaces between soil particles.

30. B

Water that soaks through the soil and carries dissolved substances into the soil is called leachate. This leachate percolates through the small spaces in the soil called pores.

31. A

Organic matter is composed of living or once-living matter. Organic matter is almost always biodegradable. Wood is biodegradable—it can be decomposed by bacteria. Some plastics can be decomposed by bacteria, but this happens so slowly that plastic can be considered non-biodegradable. Often, plastic will remain unchanged in the environment for many years.

32. B

Biodegradation is a process whereby bacteria present in the soil decompose waste products and break down complex molecules into simple substances.

33. D

Based on the data, the delegate inferred that immediately downstream from the workers' housing, the treated wastewater decreased the concentration of oxygen of the river water.

34. A

Biomagnification is the increase in the amount of harmful substances in each trophic level of the food chain. The harmful substances accumulate in the body of one organism and pass to the organism that eats it. Thus the amount of the substance increases at each level.

35. A

The symbol with a cylinder inside a circle represents compressed gas. Compressed gas is stored in cylinders.

36. C

The LD_{50} is the standard parameter used to compare the toxicity of substances. It means that when a specific dose of a toxic substance is administered to a test population, 50% of the test population will die. Generally, these tests for toxicity are carried out on rats or mice.

37. B

An MSDS does not provide information about the methods of use. It gives detailed descriptions of the product, including its composition and its chemical and physical features. It also describes how to use the product safely.

NR 2   4132

4. Raw Sewage dumped directly into a river would result in an increase in the number of bacteria needed to decompose the sewage, which would lower the oxygen levels.

1. Sulfur dioxide from the coal-burning factory would combine with water in the air to make acid, which would fall to the ground as rain or snow. The acidic moisture would eventually make its way into the river through runoff or ground water.

3. As the cattle manure was decomposed by bacteria, the phosphate that was in the manure would be released, and it would wash into the river.

2. Removing trees close to the river would expose the soil to weather elements. Heavy rains would cause the soil to erode into the river.

UNIT TEST—ENVIRONMENTAL CHEMISTRY

Use the following information to answer the next question.

A gardener is concerned with good root development in his plants in early spring.

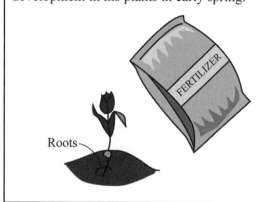

Roots

1. Which of the following elements would **not** be considered a nutrient in a bag of fertilizer?

    A. nitrogen

    B. carbon

    C. phosphorus

    D. potassium

2. Nitrogen in the air is released in a form that can chemically combine to make other usable compounds. This process is usually accomplished by bacteria and is referred to as

    A. decomposition

    B. conversion

    C. fixation

    D. uptake

3. Toxic nicotine has an LD$_{50}$ of 0.86 mg/kg. In a test sample of 1 200 rats, how many would survive this dosage?

    A. 50

    B. 220

    C. 600

    D. 1 200

4. Rapid City has a pollution problem resulting from the large number of motor vehicles used in the city. Which chemical equation represents the pollutant causing this pollution problem?

    A. $6CO_2 + 6H_2O \rightarrow C_6H_{12}O_6 + 6O_2$

    B. $2NO_2 + H_2O \rightarrow HNO_3 + HNO_2$

    C. $4Fe + 3O_2 \rightarrow 2Fe_2O_3$

    D. $2H_2 + O_2 \rightarrow 2H_2O$

5. A shipment of hydrochloric acid comes with a Materials Safety Data Sheet (MSDS). Which of the following pieces of information would not be found on the MSDS for hydrochloric acid?

    A. Source of the material

    B. Precautions to be taken

    C. A list of physical properties

    D. A description of the composition

Use the following information to answer the next question.

An organic vegetable grower notices an aphid problem that may affect his crop production. However, he is also concerned about environmental pollution.

6. What method of pest control is he most likely to use?

    A. Spraying with herbicides

    B. Fertilizing with micronutrients

    C. Introducing biological predators

    D. Watering with enzyme nutrients

Use the following diagram to answer the next question.

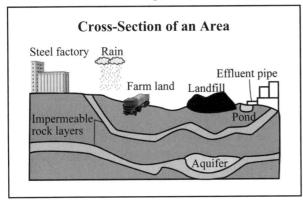

Cross-Section of an Area

7. Which of the following pollutants would **most significantly** affect the ground water aquifer in the given diagram?

A. Leachate seepage from the nearby landfill

B. Discharge of effluent into an overflow pond

C. Regular use of fertilizer during crop seeding

D. Sulfur dioxide acid rain emission from the steel factory

Use the following information to answer the next three questions.

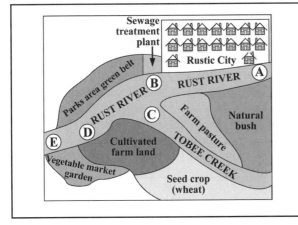

8. A sample of water was collected and tested at site **E**. It was found to have a concentration of pesticides that measured 0.055 mg/100 mL. How many ppm is this equivalent to?

A. 5.5

B. 55

C. 550

D. 5 500

Use the following additional information to answer the next question.

Another test was conducted at each of the five sites to determine the amount of suspended particles present in the water at each site. The data collected was graphed, as shown.

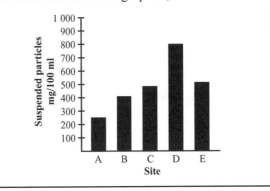

9. A possible explanation for the high amount of suspended particles at site D is

A. erosion of the cultivated land

B. aerial spraying of the wheat crop

C. irrigation of the vegetable garden

D. improper garbage disposal in the parks area

The water at each of the sites was also tested for acidity. Some of the testing was done using litmus paper. Other testing was done using a pH probe.

Site	Red Litmus	Blue Litmus	pH Reading
A	turns blue	no change	
B	no change	no change	
C			6.8
D	no change	turns red	
E			7.6

10. Which of the following rows identifies how many sites were acidic, basic, or neutral?

Row	Acidic	Basic	Neutral
A.	2	2	1
B.	1	3	1
C.	2	1	2
D.	3	1	1

11. Mucor, a saprophytic fungus, grows on decaying food material. Mucor obtains its nutrition from

  A. tree bark

  B. bread

  C. rocks

  D. water

12. Which of the following statements about water quality is **false**?

  A. In the summer, the water in a lake becomes cloudy and oxygen content is reduced.

  B. Trout are bioindicators of oxygen content in water.

  C. The clarity of the water indicates that the water is free from pollution.

  D. The presence of excessive numbers of bacteria in water may be harmful to other organisms.

Use the following information to answer the next question.

Frank was testing a sample of a liquid in science class. When a piece of blue litmus paper was placed into the liquid, the litmus paper turned red.

13. The liquid was **most likely**

  A. basic

  B. acidic

  C. a pollutant

  D. a salt solution

Use the following information to answer the next question.

DDT is a pesticide that farmers used to spray on their crops to ward off insects. Unfortunately, once DDT is released into the environment, it does not break down. Because of this, DDT can spread as shown in the given example.

crop → grasshopper → small bird → falcon

14. In this example, as the DDT passes along the food chain, the concentration of DDT would

  A. decrease then increase

  B. gradually decrease

  C. gradually increase

  D. remain the same

Use the following information to answer the next question.

The diversity of living organisms in a body of water is affected by the condition of the water. The condition of water can change over time. Scientists studying a particular pond over several years recorded changes in the water conditions, as shown in the given chart.

Condition	Changed From	Changed To
pH	4.5	6.5
Phosphate content	8 mg/L	10 mg/L
Dissolved oxygen	8 mg/L	2 mg/L
Suspended particles	12 mg/L	2 mg/L

Numerical Response

1. Indicate with a number 1 if the change in condition would have increased the biodiversity of organisms and a number 2 if the change would have decreased the biodiversity of organisms.

____	____	____	____
pH	Phosphate content	Dissolved oxygen	Suspended particles

(Record your answer as a **four-digit** number.)

Use the following information to answer the next question.

Pollutant

1. Acid rain   2. Leachate

3. Insecticide   4. Excessive phosphate

Numerical Response

2. Match each of the given pollutants with its possible source.

____	____	____	____
Sewage pond	Vehicles	Fruit orchard	Garbage dump

(Record your answer as a **four-digit** number.)

Written Response

1. Use a simple food chain example to explain the concept of biomagnification.

(2 marks)

2. Use a concept map to compare the beneficial and harmful aspects of ozone.

(2 marks)

ANSWERS AND SOLUTIONS—UNIT TEST

1. B	5. A	9. A	13. B	WR1. See Solution
2. C	6. C	10. A	14. C	WR2. See Solution
3. C	7. D	11. B	NR1. 1221	
4. B	8. C	12. C	NR2. 4132	

1. B

All of the elements except carbon are considered plant nutrients and are found in most fertilizers. The main source of carbon in plants comes from the carbon dioxide in the air.

2. C

Nitrogen fixation is the process of changing free nitrogen into nitrogen compounds that organisms can use. For example, certain bacteria located in the nodules of beans can separate nitrogen gas into free nitrogen, which then combines with other elements to form compounds such as protein.

3. C

LD stands for lethal dose. The number 50 stands for 50%. When a dose of 0.86 mg/kg is given to the test sample of rats, half will die. This means that 600 rats will survive.

4. B

Equation **A** represents photosynthesis by green plants.

Equation **C** represents the rusting or corrosion of iron.

Equation **D** represents the electrolysis of water.

All of these are natural processes and do not contribute to the pollution problem.

Equation **B** represents the production of acid rain from the release of nitrogen oxide compounds.

5. A

Composition, properties, and precautions are indicated on an MSDS. Directions for use will vary with each activity.

6. C

An organic grower would shy away from spraying with chemicals. Instead, he may introduce biological predators such as ladybugs to feed on the aphids.

7. D

An impermeable layer of rock prevents pollutants and waste material from seeping into the aquifer. Leachate from the farm, landfill, and overflow pond will be stopped by the first layer of rock. The sulfur dioxide emissions from the steel factory will mix with rain and create acid rain, which can enter the aquifer between the two layers of impermeable rocks.

8. C

The unit ppm stands for parts per million. Solve by setting up a ratio.

$$\frac{0.055}{100} = \frac{x}{1\,000\,000}$$
$$x = 550$$

9. A

Water erosion, and perhaps wind erosion, from the cultivated field along Tobee Creek and Rust River would result in more particles suspended in the water at site **D**.

10. A

Red litmus turns blue in a base. Blue litmus turns red in an acid. A pH of 7 is neutral. A pH higher than 7 is basic. A pH less than 7 is acidic.

Site	Result
A	Basic
B	Neutral
C	Acidic
D	Acidic
E	Basic

11. B

Mucor is a saprophytic fungus that grows on decaying food. It obtains nutrition from its substrate. When bread is kept in a moist, warm place, the spores of the fungus fall onto the bread and start to grow.

12. C

The clarity of water does not indicate that the water is free from pollution because clear water may contain bacteria or some dissolved pollutants.

13. B

The liquid was most likely acidic since it turned blue litmus paper red.

14. C

Because toxic substances that bioaccumulate become part of the tissues of an organism's body, they will be passed on when the organism is eaten. As these compounds are passed up through each trophic level, they accumulate in greater concentrations in the organisms of higher trophic levels. This process is called biomagnification.

NR 1   1221

A pH increase to 6.5 indicates that the water quality is becoming less acidic (more organisms). An increase in phosphate content means more plant decay and less oxygen (fewer organisms). A drop in the oxygen content results in fewer surviving organisms. A reduction in the suspended particles means clearer water with more organisms.

NR 2   4132

High nitrogen oxide emissions from vehicle exhaust cause acid rain. Leachate from the garbage material may seep into the ground water system. Insecticides can be used to control insect pests in fruit orchards. High nitrogen and phosphate content in a sewage pond may reduce the amount of oxygen available for organisms.

1. *Use a simple food chain example to explain the concept of biomagnification.*

Biomagnification refers to the increase in concentration of a chemical as it moves up through the food chain.

In a food chain such as grass → grasshopper → snake, the amount of chemical present in the snake would accumulate from the grass and the grasshopper. The concentration would be greatest in the snake and the least in the grass.

2. *Use a concept map to compare the beneficial and harmful aspects of ozone.*

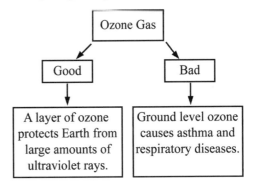

NOTES

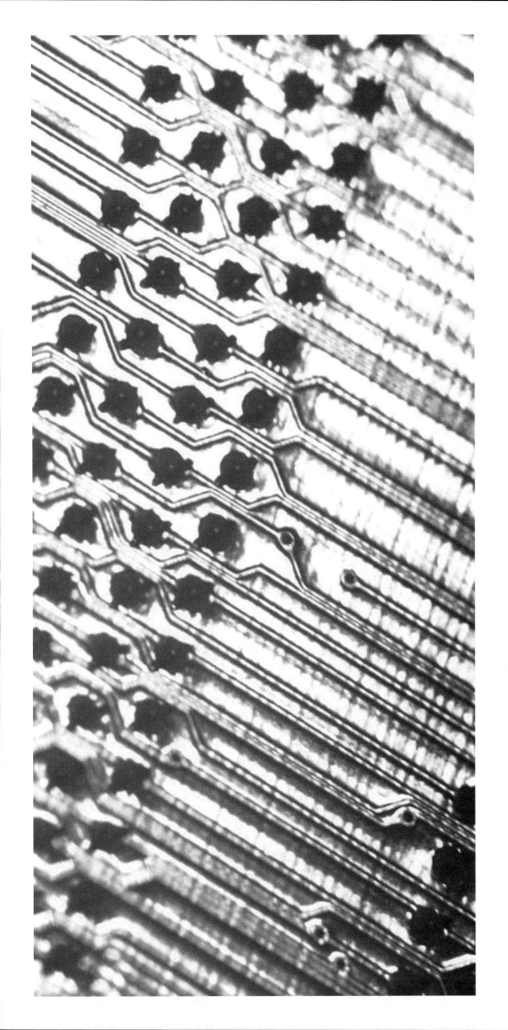

Electrical Principles
and Technologies

ELECTRICAL PRINCIPLES AND TECHNOLOGIES

Table of Correlations			
Specific Expectation	**Practice Questions**	**Unit Test Questions**	**2006 PAT**
Students will:			
D.1. *Investigate and interpret the use of devices to convert various forms of energy to electrical energy, and electrical energy to other forms of energy*			
D.1.1 identify, describe and interpret examples of mechanical, chemical, thermal, electrical and light energy	18	3	31
D.1.2 investigate and describe evidence of energy transfer and transformation	NR1, 17	4, 6	
D.1.3 investigate and evaluate the use of different electrodes, electrolytes and electrolytic concentrations in designing electrical storage cells	1	21, 22, NR1	37
D.1.4 construct, use and evaluate devices for transforming mechanical energy into electrical energy and for transforming electrical energy into mechanical energy	2, NR2	7, 11	
D.1.5 modify the design of an electrical device, and observe and evaluate resulting changes	3, 4	18	
D.2. *Describe technologies for transfer and control of electrical energy*			
D.2.1 assess the potential danger of electrical devices, by referring to the voltage and current rating (amperage) of the devices; and distinguish between safe and unsafe activities	7	16	
D.2.2 distinguish between static and current electricity, and identify example evidence of each	5	1, 2	
D.2.3 identify electrical conductors and insulators, and compare the resistance of different materials to electric flow	6		
D.2.4 use switches and resistors to control electrical flow, and predict the effects of these and other devices in given applications	9, 15	19	32
D.2.5 describe, using models, the nature of electrical current; and explain the relationship among current, resistance and voltage	10	8, 9	33, 34
D.2.6 measure voltages and amperages in circuits • *apply Ohm's law to calculate resistance, voltage and current in simple circuits*	11, 16	10	

D.2.7 develop, test and troubleshoot circuit designs for a variety of specific purposes, based on low voltage circuits	13, 14, 18, 19	14,15, NR2	35, 38
D.2.8 investigate toys, models and household appliances; and draw circuit diagrams to show the flow of electricity through them	20	17	
D.2.9 identify similarities and differences between microelectronic circuits and circuits in a house	12		36
D.3. Identify and estimate energy inputs and outputs for example devices and systems, and evaluate the efficiency of energy conversions			
D.3.1 identify the forms of energy inputs and outputs in a device or system	NR3		
D.3.2 apply appropriate units, measures and devices in determining and describing quantities of energy transformed by an electrical device, by: • measuring amperage and voltage, and calculating the number of watts consumed by an electrical device, using the formula $P = IV$ • calculating the quantity of electric energy, in joules, transformed by an electrical device, using the formula $E = P \times t$	21	12, 13, 20	
D.3.3 apply the concepts of conservation of energy and efficiency to the analysis of energy devices	24		
D.3.4 compare energy inputs and outputs of a device, and calculate its efficiency, using the formula, percentage efficiency = energy output/energy input × 100	22	WR2	
D.3.5 investigate and describe techniques for reducing waste of energy in common household devices	23		40
D.4. Describe and discuss the societal and environmental implications of the use of electrical energy			
D.4.1 identify and evaluate sources of electrical energy, including oil, gas, coal, biomass, wind and solar	25	5	
D.4.2 describe the by-products of electrical generation and their impacts on the environment	27		NR4
D.4.3 identify example uses of electrical technologies, and evaluate technologies in terms of benefits and impacts	28		
D.4.4 identify concerns regarding conservation of energy resources, and evaluate means for improving the sustainability of energy use	26	WR1	

ELECTRICAL PRINCIPLES AND TECHNOLOGIES

D.1.1   identify, describe and interpret examples of mechanical, chemical, thermal, electrical and light energy

FORMS OF ENERGY

In science, energy is defined as the ability to do work. There are many types of energy. Five common forms of energy include mechanical, chemical, thermal, electrical, and light energy.

Mechanical Energy—the energy of movement. Mechanical energy also includes the energy an object has because of its potential to move. A pendulum is a visible example of mechanical energy. A pendulum is a mass that is suspended from a point so that it can move back and forth. The mass is lifted to one side, and the stored mechanical energy changes into moving mechanical energy when the mass falls.

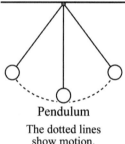

Pendulum

The dotted lines
show motion.

Chemical Energy—the energy stored in chemicals. This energy is released during chemical reactions when the chemical bonds of the compound break. Batteries use chemical energy. Food stores chemical energy, which can then be used by your body to produce movement.

Thermal Energy—the total kinetic energy of all the particles in a substance. Kinetic energy refers to how fast the particles are moving. Warm objects have more thermal energy than cool objects because the particles are moving faster. Because thermal energy refers to the total kinetic energy of a substance, 100 mL of water at 75°C will have more thermal energy than 50 mL of water at 75°C.

Electrical Energy—the energy from the flow of electrons through a conductor. The electricity produced is from the continuous movement of the electrons. Electrical energy is used in televisions, computers, and many other devices.

Light Energy—energy that travels in the form of a light wave. The most common source of light energy is the sun. Light energy allows people to see.

Practice Question: 18

D.1.2   investigate and describe evidence of energy transfer and transformation

ENERGY TRANSFER AND TRANSFORMATION

Energy can be transferred or transformed. Energy transfer occurs when one type of energy is transferred or moved from one object to another. For example, thermal energy is transferred from the stove to a frying pan through conduction. However, the type of energy does not change when energy is transferred.

Energy is transformed when it changes from one type of energy to another. When glucose is broken down in the body, chemical energy is transformed into mechanical energy for the movement of muscles and for thermal energy to keep warm. When you turn on a light bulb, electrical energy is transformed into thermal and light energy as the electrons flow through the filament of the bulb.

Energy can be neither created nor destroyed; it can only be transformed from one form to another.

Practice Questions: NR1, 17

D.1.3 *investigate and evaluate the use of different electrodes, electrolytes and electrolytic concentrations in designing electrical storage cells*

ELECTRICAL STORAGE CELLS

A cell is a commonly used device that changes chemical energy into electrical energy. This is made possible by using two different metal electrodes and an electrolyte. Within a cell, a chemical reaction occurs that releases electrons that travel from one electrode to the other. Different electrolytes and electrodes will produce cells with different properties. A cell's strength can also be changed by varying the concentration of the electrolyte used. The intended purpose of the cell will determine what kinds of electrolytes and electrodes should be used and which type of cell would be best.

There are several types of cells. **Wet cells** have liquid electrolytes, while **dry cells** use a paste. Cells that cannot be recharged are called primary cells, and rechargeable cells are called secondary cells.

Two or more cells combined together make a battery. A 12-volt car battery has six cells connected in series.

WET CELL

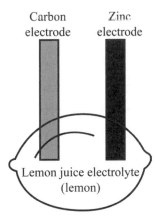

Carbon electrode   Zinc electrode

Lemon juice electrolyte (lemon)

In the given illustration of a wet cell, a chemical reaction occurs, and the electrons move from the zinc electrode (–) to the carbon electrode (+) through the electrolyte (the lemon juice).

Practice Question: 1

D.1.4 *construct, use and evaluate devices for transforming mechanical energy into electrical energy and for transforming electrical energy into mechanical energy*

D.1.5 *modify the design of an electrical device, and observe and evaluate resulting changes*

TRANSFORMING ELECTRICITY

Electricity is a form of energy that can be changed from, or into, another form of energy by technological devices.

Technological Device	Initial Energy Form	Final Energy Form
Motor	Electrical	Mechanical
Generator	Mechanical	Electrical
Thermocouple	Heat	Electrical

An **electric motor** is a device that transforms electrical energy into mechanical energy. This is made possible by the use of permanent magnets, an armature, brushes, and a split-ring commutator. Because of the continual switching of the polarity of the magnets, the armature spins.

Generators have the same basic parts as a motor, but in the case of a generator, mechanical energy is converted to electrical energy. Generators can produce direct current (DC) or alternating current (AC). The more common form of current is AC. Power companies generate AC. Power companies use high voltage (500 000 V) transmission lines to get electricity from the generating stations to your house. However, the power line going into your house is only 240 V. A **transformer** is used to step up or step down voltage depending upon the need. Inside your house, voltage is dropped again to 120 V for most appliances.

Practice Questions: 2, 3, 4, NR2

D.2.1 assess the potential danger of electrical devices, by referring to the voltage and current rating (amperage) of the devices; and distinguish between safe and unsafe activities

ELECTRICAL SAFETY

Electricity must be treated with respect at all times. Learn about the dangers of electricity and the safe practices when working with it.

Electric current is measured in amperage. Voltage is measured in volts. If either number is high, the electric current can be dangerous. Devices are required to have labels stating the necessary voltage and maximum amperage. For example, an electric mitre saw plugs into a 120 V receptacle and is rated at 15 A of current.

Become familiar with the following general rules for electrical safety:

• Know the voltage and amperage of the electricity that you work with.

• Respect high-voltage transmission lines. Transmission lines carry extremely high voltage current.

• Do not plug any electrical device into a wall outlet if the cords are damaged in any way, if the wires are exposed, or if the third prong (the ground) has been broken or removed from the plug.

• Avoid mixing water and electricity in all circumstances.

• If you are working with electricity coming from a wall outlet, be aware that this amount of electricity can cause serious bodily harm. Avoid standing in water or touching metal plumbing pipes, metal countertops, or any other conductors that could cause the electricity to pass through your body while working with electricity.

Practice Question: 7

D.2.2 distinguish between static and current electricity, and identify example evidence of each

ELECTRIC CURRENT

Atoms build up a charge by losing or gaining electrons. An atom that loses electrons becomes positively charged. An atom that gains electrons becomes negatively charged. The behaviour of charged objects can be predicted according to the **law of electrical charge**. This behaviour is shown in the following chart:

Objects with opposite charges attract each other	$+ \rightarrow \leftarrow -$
Objects with the same charges repel each other	$+ \leftrightarrow +$

Static electricity occurs when two objects with opposite electrical charges come close enough to each other to allow electrons to move from the negatively charged object to the positively charged one. This electron movement is the cause of the shock a person felt or the zap heard or spark seen as the charged objects return to a neutral condition. A lightning flash is a very large discharge of static electricity.

Unlike static electricity, which occurs randomly, current electricity is predictable. **Current electricity** is the movement of electrons along a conducting path. For example, current electricity moves along copper wire.

Practice Question: 5

D.2.3 identify electrical conductors and insulators, and compare the resistance of different materials to electric flow

CONDUCTORS, INSULATORS, AND RESISTORS

Conductors allow for the movement of electricity, whereas **insulators** oppose the movement. **Resistors** allow some, but not all, of the current to pass through. Current passing through a resistor can produce heat and light. Resistance is what makes a light bulb or a stove element work. Common examples of conductors, insulators, and resistors are listed as follows:

• Conductor—copper and aluminum

• Insulator—plastic and rubber

• Resistor—tungsten filament and heater element

Practice Question: 6

D.2.4 use switches and resistors to control electrical flow, and predict the effects of these and other devices in given applications

CONTROLLING ELECTRICAL FLOW

A switch can be used to control the flow of electricity through a circuit by turning it on or off. When the switch is open, the conducting points are not in contact with each other, and no current can flow through. When the switch is closed, however, the conducting points are connected, and current can flow through the system. That is why the light in a room will turn on when the light switch is set to "on."

Resistance in an electric circuit is a measure of how easily the current flows. A resistor in a circuit is similar to a water pipe with a small diameter. Water flowing in a narrow pipe has more resistance than water flowing in a wide pipe. Because the resistor makes it more difficult for current to flow though, the voltage (or pressure) drops as it flows through the resistor. Components such as bulbs and motors act as resistors in a circuit.

Practice Questions: 9, 15

D.2.5 describe, using models, the nature of electrical current; and explain the relationship among current, resistance and voltage

CURRENT, RESISTANCE, AND VOLTAGE

Current, resistance, and voltage are related to each other. The voltage of a system depends directly upon the current and resistance in a circuit. Think of pouring some water from a bucket through a tube. If you pour water from a bucket 1 m from the ground, it has less potential energy than if you pour water from the same bucket from a height of 10 m. The height of the bucket is like voltage. The amount of water flowing from the bucket is like current. A large amount of water poured out from a bucket demonstrates a large current. A small amount poured out demonstrates a small current. Resistance refers to how easily current can flow. If instead of wide tubing, a piece of narrow tubing is used, the amount of water that can flow through the tubing is much less.

The narrower path creates more resistance. Because the resistance is high, not as much water (or current) can flow. Therefore, as resistance increases, current decreases.

Practice Question: 10

D.2.6   *measure voltages and amperages
        in circuits*

- *apply Ohm's law to calculate resistance,
  voltage and current in simple circuits*

ELECTRICAL TERMS

The relationship between the current, voltage and resistance in a circuit is described by Ohm's Law using the terms listed in the table.

Electrical Term	Definition	Unit of Measurement	Symbol
Current	Rate of flow	Ampere (A)	I
Voltage	Force of flow	Volt (V)	V
Resistance	Obstacle to flow	Ohm (Ω)	R

OHM'S LAW

Ohm's Law states that the voltage of a system is directly related to the current multiplied by the resistance:

V=IR

When one term changes, there must be a change in one or both of the others. The formula can be written to calculate voltage, resistance, or current.

$$V = I \times R$$
$$R = \frac{V}{I}$$
$$I = \frac{V}{R}$$

V = Voltage
I = Current
R = Resistance

Example

An electric heater uses 12 A of electricity when plugged into a 120 V outlet. What is the resistance of the heater?

Solution

$$R = \frac{V}{I}$$
$$= \frac{120 \text{ V}}{12 \text{ A}}$$
$$= 10 \ \Omega$$

Practice Questions: 11, 16

D.2.7   *develop, test and troubleshoot circuit
        designs for a variety of specific purposes,
        based on low voltage circuits*

D.2.8   *investigate toys, models and household
        appliances; and draw circuit diagrams to
        show the flow of electricity through them*

CIRCUITS

An electrical circuit is a system made up of four subsystems.

Source: Cell or battery
Conductor: Wire
Control: Switch
Load: Lamp or motor

When the switch is turned off and the current is interrupted, the circuit is said to be **open**. When the switch is on, allowing for the flow of current, the switch is **closed**.

If a simple circuit consisting of a cell connected to a switch and a light does not work, troubleshooting can possibly determine the cause. Troubleshooting involves checking to see if the cell is dead, the light is burnt out, or if the wires are improperly connected.

Electrical circuits can be set up as series circuits or as parallel circuits.

A series circuit is a circuit with one path of electron flow.	A parallel circuit is a circuit with multiple paths of electron flow.
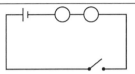	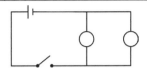
The voltage in this cell is shared by the two light bulbs, which causes the second bulb to be dimmer than the first. If one bulb burns out, the other will not work.	The voltage in this cell is shared equally by the two light bulbs. The bulbs will burn equally bright. If one bulb burns out, the other will still work.

Practice Questions: 13, 14, 18, 19, 20

D.2.9   identify similarities and differences between microelectronic circuits and circuits in a house

COMPARING CIRCUITS WITH MICROELECTRONIC CIRCUITS

Microcircuits, or integrated circuits are used in televisions and computers. These circuits differ in size from circuits that carry electricity throughout a house and use much less current and voltage. Microcircuits are extremely small and contain microscopic transistors and resistors. More than a million components can be placed on a chip that is no larger than one square centimetre. A transistor is often used instead of a switch in a microcircuit. Transistors have no moving parts and can be made much smaller than traditional switches used in homes.

Practice Question: 12

D.3.1   identify the forms of energy inputs and outputs in a device or system

D.3.4   compare energy inputs and outputs of a device, and calculate its efficiency, using the formula, percentage efficiency = energy output/energy input × 100

INPUT, OUTPUT, AND EFFICIENCY

Input refers to the amount of energy put into a device, and **output** refers to the amount of energy that comes out. A device may change the type of energy but not the amount. For example, a light bulb's input energy is in the form of electrical energy, and its output energy is in the form of light and heat energy.

EFFICIENCY

Efficiency is the ratio of useful energy that comes out of a device to the total energy that went into it. Remember that energy cannot be destroyed, but it can be converted from one form to another.

$$\% \text{ efficiency} = \frac{\text{output}}{\text{input}} \times 100\%$$

Example

What is the efficiency of an incandescent light bulb that releases 62 kJ of light energy from an input of 1 560 kJ of total energy?

Solution

$$\% \text{ efficiency} = \frac{62 \text{ kJ}}{1\ 560 \text{ kJ}} \times 100$$
$$= 4\%$$

The incandescent light bulb is 4% efficient in producing light and wastes 96% of the input energy in the form of heat. It is very inefficient. A fluorescent bulb is more efficient than an incandescent bulb.

Practice Questions: NR3, 22

D.3.2 *apply appropriate units, measures and devices in determining and describing quantities of energy transformed by an electrical device, by:*

- *measuring amperage and voltage, and calculating the number of watts consumed by an electrical device, using the formula* $P = I \times V$
- *calculating the quantity of electric energy, in joules, transformed by an electrical device using the formula* $E = P \times t$

POWER AND ENERGY

Power, measured in watts, is the rate at which a device converts energy. Power is dependent on the current rating of an appliance and the voltage passing through it. Power is calculated using the following equation.

power (watts) = current rating (amps) × voltage (volts)
$$P = I \times V$$

Example

What is the power rating in watts (W) of a curling iron that plugs into a 120 V circuit and uses 9 A of current?

Solution

$P = I \times V$
$P = 9\ A \times 120\ V$
$P = 1080\ W$

Energy (E) is dependent on power (P) and time (t). Energy is calculated using the following equation.

E (joules) = P (watts) × t (sec)

Challenge: How much energy is used by a 4 A appliance that is plugged into a 120 V circuit for 4 min?

Step 1
Calculate the power used.
$P = I \times V$
$\quad = 4\ A \times 120\ V$
$\quad = 480\ W$

Step 2
Calculate the energy used.
$E = P \times t$
$\quad = 480\ W \times 4\ min \times 60\ s/min$
$\quad = 115\ 200\ J$

Producing and distributing electricity is expensive. Power companies pass their costs on to the consumer and charge per kilowatt hour of use.

Example

What is the cost of operating a 2 400 W heater two hours per day for a 20-day period? The charge per kilowatt hour is $0.10.

Solution

Step 1
Change watts to kilowatts.
$$\frac{2\ 400\ W}{1\ 000} = 2.4\ kW$$

Step 2
Multiply by the hours of use.
2.4 kW × 2 h = 4.8 kWh

Step 3
Multiply by the days of use.
4.8 kWh × 20 = 96 kWh

Step 4
Multiply by the cost per kilowatt hour.
96 kWh × $0.10 = $9.60

Practice Question: 21

D.3.3 apply the concepts of conservation of energy and efficiency to the analysis of energy devices

ANALYZING ENERGY DEVICES

The law of conservation of energy states that energy can be neither created nor destroyed; it can only be transformed. When efficiencies of energy devices are examined, there is sometimes much more energy put into the device than is converted into a useful form of energy. The energy that has been lost is often lost in the form of heat as a result of friction. All mechanical devices will lose some useful energy because energy dissipates to the surroundings in the form of heat.

Many new models of appliances are more energy efficient than they were in the past. They are better designed and better insulated than previous models. Such appliances must carry EnerGuide labels that indicate their energy consumption ratings.

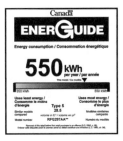

Practice Question: 24

D.3.5 investigate and describe techniques for reducing waste of energy in common household devices

CONSERVING ELECTRICAL ENERGY

There are several simple things that you can do at home or in school to help cut back on energy usage:

- When leaving a room, turn off the lights.

- Replace incandescent light bulbs with fluorescent bulbs.

- Wash the dishes by hand instead of using the dishwasher.

- Hang wet clothes on a clothesline instead of using a clothes dryer.

- Turn off computers and the television when they are not being used.

- Use air conditioners only when necessary.

- Turn down the heat at night or when people are out of the house during the day.

Practice Question: 23

D.4.1 identify and evaluate sources of electrical energy, including oil, gas, coal, biomass, wind and solar

ENERGY SOURCES

Much of the world's electricity is generated from coal and uranium. These energy sources are slowly becoming depleted. Consequently, the search is on to find alternative forms of energy. Wind, tides, and steam (geothermal energy) are now being harnessed to produce electricity. Scientists are investigating how to produce electricity from solar panels and fuel cells.

Whatever energy form is used, caution must be exercised to ensure that the environment is not seriously affected and that natural resources are being used sustainably.

Practice Question: 25

D.4.2 describe the by-products of electrical generation and their impacts on the environment

ELECTRICITY AND THE ENVIRONMENT

Fossil fuels, such as gas and coal, which are used to generate electricity have an impact on the environment. Byproducts of coal-generated power cause pollution and global warming. The carbon dioxide, sulfur dioxide, and nitrogen oxide emitted into the atmosphere cause the greenhouse effect and produce acid rain. While there are environmental costs to the production of more "green" sources of energy, such as the land that must be available for wind harnessing or the fish that may be affected by dams for tidal energy, these sources of energy are much less harmful to the environment than the burning of fossil fuels.

Practice Question: 27

D.4.3 identify example uses of electrical technologies, and evaluate technologies in terms of benefits and impacts

ELECTRICAL TECHNOLOGIES

Cellphones, computers, MP3 players, dishwashers, and televisions are just some of the electrical technologies people use every day. While these devices have many benefits to society, there are some costs associated with them. To assess the environmental impact of a specific technology, the impact of the manufacturing, daily usage, and disposal of the technology need to be considered.

Manufacturing computers, for example, requires a lot of energy. Most of this energy is produced by burning fossil fuels, which contributes to the greenhouse effect and climate change. Along with the energy required, the manufacturing process uses a lot of materials and chemicals.

Because computer technology changes so quickly, computers quickly become outdated.

These outdated machines are thrown out, resulting in large piles of computer equipment in landfills. New recycling facilities reduce the amount of electronic materials that end up in landfills, but the recycling process also requires energy from fossil fuels.

Practice Question: 28

D.4.4 identify concerns regarding conservation of energy resources, and evaluate means for improving the sustainability of energy use

ENERGY CONSERVATION AND SUSTAINABILITY

Fossil fuels are a non-renewable energy source. This means that people need to conserve these resources to prevent them from being depleted too quickly. There are many things to consider when deciding how to conserve energy. For example, an electric car does not burn gasoline; however, the electricity that it uses may have been generated by burning fossil fuels.

When resources are replenished at the same rate as they are used, they are said to be **sustainable**. This concept may include conserving the current non-renewable resources so they are available for long periods of time. It could also mean that non-renewable resources such as fossil fuels are not used at all because they cannot be replenished. Some sustainable choices people are making include riding bikes to work instead of driving, purchasing high-efficiency appliances, and turning lights off when they leave a room.

Practice Question: 26

PRACTICE QUESTIONS—ELECTRICAL PRINCIPLES AND TECHNOLOGIES

Use the following information to answer the next question.

Cam and his lab partner, Eden, were assigned the task of determining the energy conversion that occurs in four different devices.

D cell
Cell

Generator

Motor

Steel Copper

Thermocouple

A list of several types of energy conversions was posted on the whiteboard.

1. Mechanical to electrical

2. Electrical to heat

3. Electrical to chemical

4. Electrical to mechanical

5. Chemical to electrical

6. Heat to electrical

Numerical Response

1. Match each device with the energy conversion that takes place in it.

____ ____ ____ ____

Cell   Generator   Motor   Thermocouple

(Record your answer as a **four-digit** number.)

Use the following information to answer the next question.

Students have chosen the best electrodes to use in an experiment in order to determine the best electrolyte. Using each of the electrolytes in turn, the students connected their cell to a light bulb and judged how bright the light was.

1. For this experiment, the manipulated, responding, and controlled variables are the
   A. bulb brightness, type of electrolyte, and metal electrodes, respectively
   B. type of electrolyte, bulb brightness, and metal electrodes, respectively
   C. metal electrodes, type of electrolyte, and bulb brightness, respectively
   D. type of electrolyte, metal electrodes, and bulb brightness, respectively

Use the following information to answer the next question.

The following list describes characteristics that apply to either direct current or alternating current.

1. Flows in one direction only

2. Flows in a back and forth direction

3. Makes a ccll phone work

4. Makes a toaster work

2. Which of the given characteristics apply to direct current?
   A. 1 and 2
   B. 1 and 3
   C. 2 and 3
   D. 2 and 4

Use the following information to answer the next two questions.

Katie and Miroslav are given the task of building an electric motor for their science class. They are to investigate the properties of their motor and determine ways in which they can change its performance. The design they finally settle on is illustrated in the given diagram.

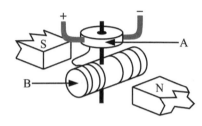

3. The parts of the motor labelled A and B are the

   A. rotor and spindle, respectively

   B. armature and rotor, respectively

   C. spindle and commutator, respectively

   D. commutator and armature, respectively

4. Miroslav wants to make the motor spin faster without using more voltage. He can do this by

   A. making more splits in the metal of part A

   B. increasing the number of turns of wire on part B

   C. decreasing the strength of the fixed side magnets

   D. changing to a power supply with more electrical output

Use the following information to answer the next question.

When balloons *X* and *Y* were suspended from the ceiling in a science classroom, they moved away from each other.

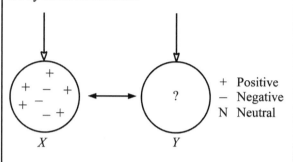

5. For the two balloons to repel each other, balloon *Y* **most likely** has which of the following electrical charges?

   A.

   B.

   C.

   D.

Use the following information to answer the next question.

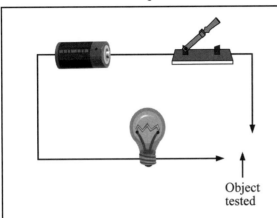

Object
tested

In science class, students tested different objects to determine whether they would complete a circuit and make the bulb light up. The following objects were tested:

I. A glass rod

II. Aluminum foil

III. An iron paper clip

IV. A plastic spoon

6. Which of the objects tested will make the bulb light up?
   A. I and II
   B. I and IV
   C. II and III
   D. II and IV

Use the following information to answer the next three questions.

Several students from Yorktown Junior High School entered a competition at the local science fair. One part of the competition was to design the fastest electric-powered car. The rules stated that the judges would disqualify any cars deemed unsafe. There were four entries in this competition.

I. A battery-powered car with a motor attached directly to a wheel

II. A solar-powered car powered by the light in the room

III. A car with a long extension cord that plugged into a wall socket

IV. A car powered by batteries and controlled by a radio-controlled remote control unit also powered by batteries.

7. The entry **most likely** to be disqualified on the basis of safety is car
   A. I
   B. II
   C. III
   D. IV

8. Energy is transferred in car I from
   A. mechanical to light to electrical
   B. light to electrical to mechanical
   C. sound to mechanical to electrical
   D. chemical to electrical to mechanical

9. What would be the effect of adding an extra resistor to the circuit between the batteries and the motor of car I?
   A. The battery would melt.
   B. The voltage would increase.
   C. The motor would slow down.
   D. The wires would become very hot.

Use the following information to answer the next question.

In an attempt to show an understanding of how current, resistance, and voltage are related, John and Tia drew the following diagram.

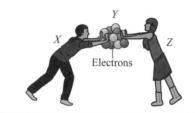

10. From the given diagram, it can be concluded that *X*, *Y*, and *Z* represent

   A. current, voltage, and resistance, respectively

   B. voltage, resistance, and current, respectively

   C. voltage, current, and resistance, respectively

   D. current, resistance, and voltage, respectively

Use the following information to answer the next question.

On a demonstration table, there are two wire coils, each with a different number of wire turns, a selection of connecting wires, a bar magnet, and a galvanometer. The galvanometer is connected to each of the coils in turn, and the magnet is moved toward the coil with the speed indicated in the given chart.

Coil *A*   Coil *B*

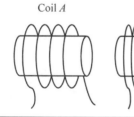

Trial	Coil	**Speed of Magnet**
1	*A*	Slow
2	*B*	Slow
3	*A*	Fast
4	*B*	Fast

11. Which of the given trials will produce the **most** current in the galvanometer?

   A. 1

   B. 2

   C. 3

   D. 4

12. A transistor is often referred to as a solid state component with no moving parts. Transistors are found in microcircuits and function as

   A. loads

   B. switches

   C. conductors

   D. sources of power

Use the following information to answer the next four questions.

Sam was asked to find out what was wrong with the motorized windmill that his friends made for science class. The windmill is shown in the given illustration.

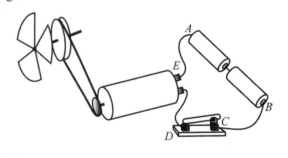

13. While troubleshooting the circuit, Sam noticed that a voltmeter reads zero when the wire is connected to points *A* and *B*. This **most likely** means that the

   A. wire from *B* to *C* is defective

   B. motor is broken inside

   C. batteries are dead

   D. switch is open

14. After correcting the problem, the voltmeter connected to points *A* and *B* reads 3.0 V. The motor does not work when the switch is closed. Which of the following explanations is **not** a possible reason why the motor does not run?

    A. A wire may be defective.

    B. The motor might be dead.

    C. The switch may not work.

    D. The connection between the two cells might be broken.

15. Sam fixed the circuit but found that the windmill spun too fast. He could slow the speed of the windmill by

    A. replacing the pulley on the motor's armature with one that has a larger diameter

    B. replacing the pulley on the windmill's vanes with one that has a smaller diameter

    C. adding another battery to the circuit

    D. adding a resistor to the circuit

Use the following additional information to answer the next question.

After replacing the circuit, Sam checked the voltage using the given voltmeter.

16. What voltage was passing though the circuit Sam repaired?

    A. 6.00 V

    B. 2.4 V

    C. 2.1 V

    D. 1.6 V

Use the following information to answer the next question.

Ed and Sally have a small vacation cabin. They attached a small generator to a water wheel in the creek to create electricity for the cabin.

17. In order, the energy transfer in their system is

    A. electrical to mechanical to gravitational

    B. gravitational to electrical to mechanical

    C. mechanical to gravitational to electrical

    D. gravitational to mechanical to electrical

Use the following additional information to answer the next two questions.

Ed and Sally rigged up lights in their cabin.

18. Which of the following circuits would allow each person to turn his or her own light on and off?

A.

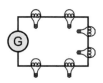

B.

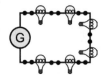

C.

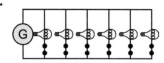

D.

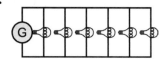

19. Ed and Sally found that the reading lights were too dim at night. Which of the following strategies would solve this problem?

A. Adding a resistor between the generator and the lights

B. Slowing down the water wheel attached to the generator

C. Speeding up the water wheel attached to the generator

D. Using bulbs that require less voltage to run

Use the following information to answer the next question.

Imelda designed a circuit to a door alarm that controls a light and a radio.

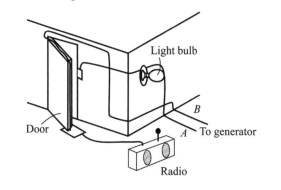

20. This circuit is designed in such a way that it will

A. play the radio and turn on the light when the door is opened

B. play the radio and turn off the light when the door is opened

C. turn off both the radio and the light when the door is opened

D. turn off the radio and turn on the light when the door is opened

Use the following information to answer the next question.

Allie was asked to research how a direct current (DC) generator compares with an alternating current (AC) generator. She recorded a list of facts about these two forms of current.

I. Current commonly produced in the charging system in cars

II. Current produced travels in one direction.

III. Current produced with two split-ring commutators and two contact points

IV. Current produced changes direction and travels in cycles.

Numerical Response

2. Write the number 1 in the blank if the fact pertains to DC generators and the number 2 in the blank if the fact pertains to AC generators.

___ ___ ___ ___
 I   II   III   IV

(Record your answer as a **four-digit** number.)

Use the following information to answer the next question.

Electrical consumption in an older home is generally measured by a dial meter in kilowatt hours. At a particular house, readings were taken on September 30 and October 31.

September 30

October 31

Numerical Response

3. The total electrical consumption for the one-month period (September 30 to October 31) was _____ kWh. (Record your answer as a **five-digit** number.)

21. What electrical concept is the term *watt* associated with?

A. Power   B. Current

C. Voltage   D. Resistance

Use the following information to answer the next question.

Most of the energy produced by an incandescent light bulb is wasted as heat. The light bulb is only 4% efficient in producing light.

22. If 800 J of input energy went into producing light, what is the output energy the bulb capable of?

A. 10 J   B. 24 J

C. 32 J   D. 63 J

Use the following information to answer the next question.

All large appliances sold in Canada must display the EnerGuide symbol rating the energy consumption and efficiency of the appliance.

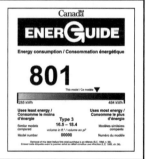

23. The number 801 on the EnerGuide label in the given illustration indicates that the appliance uses 801

A. joules per month

B. kWh per month

C. joules per year

D. kWh per year

Use the following information to answer the next question.

An electric motor and a car's internal combustion engine are tested in a lab for power output and input.

24. Both engines put out 80 horsepower, but the efficiency of the electric motor is greater because

A. it costs less to manufacture

B. electricity is a cheaper source of energy than fuel

C. fewer moving parts means less friction is produced

D. the movement of its parts is at a lower RPM (revolutions per minute)

Use the following information to answer the next question.

A power plant is located near a sanitary landfill site. The garbage brought in daily is covered and eventually decomposes, producing methane gas.

25. The methane gas that is produced from decaying garbage is referred to as

A. biochemical waste

B. bioenergy

C. biomass

D. biocycle

26. Methane gas at a landfill site is collected by a network of underground pipes and transported to a power-generating station. This technique of making methane gas from garbage and then using the methane gas as fuel to generate electricity is referred to as a

A. binary system

B. multi-use system

C. cooperative system

D. cogeneration system

27. Electrical power is generated using different sources of energy. Which of the following sources of energy produces the **most** pollution?

A. Coal

B. Wind

C. Water

D. Sunlight

28. Which of the following events is **not** an indirect environmental consequence of the increasing use of computers?

A. The use of computers can cause repetitive strain injuries.

B. Discarded computers might leak toxins into the landfill.

C. The production of computers uses a lot of energy from fossil fuels.

D. Computers use electricity while they are turned on, even if they are on standby.

ANSWERS AND SOLUTIONS—PRACTICE QUESTIONS

NR1. 5146	**8. D**	**16. D**	**22. C**
1. B	**9. C**	**17. D**	**23. D**
2. B	**10. C**	**18. C**	**24. C**
3. D	**11. D**	**19. C**	**25. B**
4. B	**12. B**	**20. B**	**26. D**
5. A	**13. C**	**NR2. 2122**	**27. A**
6. C	**14. D**	**NR3. 13 073**	**28. A**
7. C	**15. D**	**21. A**	

NR 1   5146

A chemical reaction between the electrodes and the electrolyte in a cell produces a flow of electrons.
A rotating generator, such as the type used in a hydroelectric power plant, produces energy by converting mechanical energy to electricity.
A motor, on the other hand, must have an electrical source to make it work. A motor converts electrical energy into mechanical energy.
"Thermo" means heat. A thermocouple is a device consisting of two different metals that converts heat energy into electrical energy.

1.   B

The students manipulate the type of electrolyte they are using, and the bulb responds by changing brightness. The metal electrodes are kept constant so that they do not influence the voltage produced.

2.   B

The battery in a cellphone produces a current that flows in one direction. This is an example of a direct current.

3.   D

This motor makes use of a split-ring commutator (labelled A), and the spinning electromagnet is referred to as the armature (labelled B).

4.   B

To produce more force between the armature (electromagnet) and the fixed magnets, Miroslav must increase the magnetic field of either the armature or the fixed magnets. In this case, adding more coils has the effect of making a stronger electromagnet.

5.   A

Balloon X is positively charged because it has more protons (+) than electrons (–). The law of electrical charges states that like charges repel. A negative charge will repel a negative charge, and a positive charge will repel a positive charge. The positively charged balloon Y will repel the positively charged balloon X.

6.   C

Metallic objects are conductors of electricity. Aluminum foil and the iron paper clip will permit electrons to flow easily. Glass and plastic are insulators. They prevent electrical current from passing through.

7.   C

Car III runs on household current that could be potentially lethal if handled incorrectly.
This would be a serious safety issue that would likely result in the entry being disqualified.

8. D

The battery converts chemical energy into electrical energy that in turn is converted into the mechanical energy that drives the wheels.

9. C

Adding a resistor would slow down the motor, since the resistor would reduce the amount of current delivered to the motor.

10. C

Voltage, sometimes called potential difference, is the force needed to make electrons move. This force is represented by *X*. *Y* represents the number of particles that are being moved. This is referred to as current. *Z* opposes this movement of particles by providing the resistance.

11. D

The amount of current generated depends on the amount of wire used and the speed of the magnet relative to the wire. Trial 4 has a fast magnet and a large spool of wire. A fast-moving magnet though a large number of coils produces the greatest current.

12. B

Most transistors are constructed with three layers of treated silicon. Usually, the middle layer controls the current and, like a switch, allows a small voltage to pass through.

13. C

A reading of zero means there is no flow of electricity between points *A* and *B*. A reading of zero here means that the batteries are dead. There may be other problems in the circuit. However, in order to test for them, the batteries would first have to be replaced, and then the voltmeter leads could be moved to different points on the circuit.

14. D

The voltmeter shows that the batteries are functioning, but the motor does not run. The connection between the batteries must be okay because otherwise, the voltmeter would not show a reading across points *A* and *B*. Possible reasons that the motor does not run include that the wire is broken, that the switch does not work, or that the motor is defective.

15. D

A resistor will decrease the amount of current supplied to the circuit. This will slow the motor down and will ultimately slow the windmill down. Replacing the pulley on the motor's armature with one that has a larger diameter, replacing the pulley on the windmill's vanes with one that has a smaller diameter, and adding another battery to the circuit will all cause the windmill to turn faster.

16. D

The meter has a maximum reading of 3 V. The needle is positioned slightly more than halfway between 1 V and 2 V. The best estimated reading is 1.6 V.

17. D

Gravitational energy is required to get the water flowing. As the water flows past the water wheel, it turns the wheel (mechanical energy), and the movement of the generator converts that energy into electrical energy.

18. C

Circuits A and D have no switches. In circuit B, turning off a switch turns all the lights off. The design of circuit C allows each person to have his or her light operating independently of the other person's light.

19. C

Adding a resistor, slowing down the water wheel, and using lower voltage bulbs would all have the effect of making the lights dimmer. Speeding up the water wheel would increase the amount of power generated and therefore make the lights brighter.

20. B

Referring to the diagram of Imelda's current: as the door opens, the contact with the light is opened and the contact with the radio is closed. The radio will start playing, and the light will go off. When the door is closed, the electricity flows to the light. When the door is open, electricity flows to the radio.

NR 2   2122

DC generators (sometimes called dynamos) have one split-ring commutator and produce a current in one direction. AC generators are slightly different in that a loop of wire is attached to two split rings.

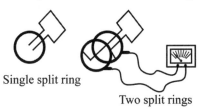

Single split ring

Two split rings

A car's charging system has an alternator that changes the direction of an electrical current.

NR 3   13 073

The dial reading for September 30 is 10 767 kWh. The dial reading for October 31 is 23 840 kWh.

The difference is 13 073 kWh.

21. A

A watt is a measure of electrical power. One watt is equivalent to one joule per second of energy. The number of watts of power can be determined in several ways.

I. Power (watts) $= \dfrac{E \text{ (joules)}}{t \text{ (seconds)}}$

II. Power (watts) $= V$ (volts) $\times I$ (current in amps)

22. C

$$4\% = \frac{4}{100}$$

$$\% \text{ Efficiency} = \frac{\text{Output Energy}}{\text{Input Energy}} \times 100$$

$$\frac{4}{100} = \frac{\text{OE}}{800 \text{ J}}$$

$$100 \text{ OE} = 4 \times 800 \text{ J}$$

$$100 \text{ OE} = 3\,200 \text{ J}$$

$$\text{OE} = 32 \text{ J}$$

23. D

The EnerGuide rating for this appliance is 801 kWh/year. This means that under standard conditions, the appliance will use an average of 801 kWh of power during one year's use. At a rate of $0.10/kWh, it would cost $80.10 to operate the appliance for an entire year.

24. C

In an electric motor, the armature is the only moving part. Fewer moving parts mean less wasted energy as a result of friction. Less wasted energy results in greater efficiency.

25. B

Bioenergy is the useful energy that is generated by decomposing garbage.

Biochemical waste is a specific type of waste produced through industrial or biological processes.

The term *biocycle* refers to the biological cycles that occur within an organism or within an ecosystem.

26. D

The term *cogeneration* refers to an efficient technology that produces two or more forms of energy that can be put to alternative uses. Garbage (biomass) produces fuel, and the fuel is burned to produce electrical power.

27. A

Burning coal to generate electricity produces carbon dioxide, sulfur oxide, and nitrogen oxide emissions. These emissions contribute to global warming and acid rain problems.

28. A

While computer use can cause repetitive strain injuries, this is not an environmental consequence.

UNIT TEST—ELECTRICAL PRINCIPLES AND TECHNOLOGIES

Use the following information to answer the next question.

Two balloons become charged after being rubbed with different cloth materials.

Balloon 1   **Balloon 2**

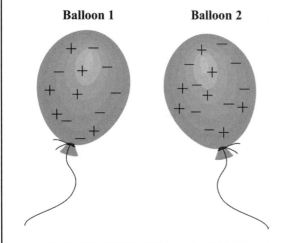

1. What will happen if balloon 1 is brought near balloon 2?

   A. Balloon 1 will repel Balloon 2.

   B. Balloon 1 will attract Balloon 2.

   C. Balloon 1 will fuse with Balloon 2.

   D. Balloon 1 will have no effect on Balloon 2.

2. When Tia removed a load of clothes from the dryer, she noticed that all the sweaters stuck together. This is an example of

   A. static electricity produced by like charges

   B. current electricity produced by neutral objects

   C. static electricity produced by unlike charges

   D. current electricity produced by the conducting clothes

Use the following information to answer the next question.

A team of students constructed a solar-powered car for their science fair project. The car was made by hooking up the car assembly to a motor and a solar panel. During the initial test trial, the car travelled the length of a well-lit room.

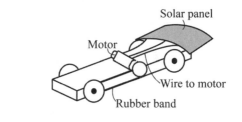

3. In travelling across the room, the car converted

   A. solar energy into mechanical energy into electrical energy

   B. solar energy into potential energy into electrical energy

   C. solar energy into thermal energy into chemical energy

   D. solar energy into electrical energy into mechanical energy

Use the following information to answer the next question.

The following illustration shows equipment used to trigger an explosion.

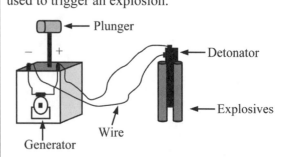

4. The energy conversions that take place from the time the plunger is pushed down to the time the explosives detonate are from

A. electrical to mechanical to chemical

B. mechanical to electrical to chemical

C. chemical to electrical to mechanical

D. mechanical to chemical to electrical

Source: PAT, 1999

5. Iceland is located in an area where two of Earth's tectonic plates meet. The splitting of the plates creates a natural energy source referred to as

A. wind power

B. tidal power

C. solar power

D. geothermal power

Use the following information to answer the next question.

A cabin in a remote mountain area is lit using wind as an energy source.

6. The energy conversion taking place to light the cabin is

A. electrical to light to mechanical

B. mechanical to light to electrical

C. electrical to mechanical to light

D. mechanical to electrical to light

Use the following information to answer the next question.

Devices such as MP3 players, computers, and calculators use a current that flows in one direction.

7. The given current is referred to as

A. direct current

B. inductive current

C. alternating current

D. electromagnetic current

Use the following information to answer the next question.

A 100 W incandescent light bulb has a tungsten filament that resists the flow of an electrical current producing light and heat. The resistance of the tungsten filament is dependent on the characteristics of the wire used in the filament.

8. Which of the following types of tungsten wire will offer the **most** resistance?

A. A short, thick wire

B. A long, thick wire

C. A short, thin wire

D. A long, thin wire

Use the following information to answer the next question.

A science class performed an experiment to determine the effect of a wire length and thickness on its resistance.

Four different sizes of Nichrome wire were tested.

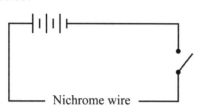

Nichrome wire

Wire	Length (cm)	Thickness (mm)
1	12	2
2	8	1
3	12	1
4	8	2

9. Which of the given wires would produce the **lowest** ohmmeter reading when connected to a battery of three cells?

   A. Wire 1

   B. Wire 2

   C. Wire 3

   D. Wire 4

10. A standard 120 V electrical outlet can handle a maximum of 15 A of current. If an appliance with a resistance of 12 Ω is plugged in, how many amperes of current are available for another appliance?

   A. 3

   B. 5

   C. 10

   D. 12

Use the following information to answer the next question.

A galvanometer is an instrument that uses a magnetic needle in an electrical field to detect small currents of electricity.

11. In order to measure the electric current in a circuit, a galvanometer is connected

   A. in series to the circuit

   B. in parallel to the circuit

   C. at any point in the circuit

   D. near the cell in the circuit

12. What information is required to calculate electrical power?

   A. Current and time

   B. Time and voltage

   C. Current and voltage

   D. Voltage and displacement

13. A bulb is provided with 60 W of electrical power. How much energy does the 60 W bulb use in 1 min?

   A. 6 J

   B. 60 J

   C. 360 J

   D. 3 600 J

Use the following information to answer the next question.

A circuit was constructed according to the following schematic diagram.

Characteristics of the Circuit

1. L_1—burnt out

2. S_1—closed

3. S_2—open

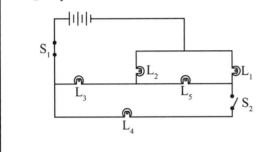

14. If the three characteristics were considered in this circuit, which lamps would continue to light?

   A. Only L_2

   B. L_2 and L_3

   C. L_2, L_3, and L_5

   D. L_2, L_3, and L_4

Use the following information to answer the next question.

The director on a movie set must to be able to turn a special-effect light off and on from two different locations. An electrician drew a circuit diagram using the symbols shown in the following illustration.

 G   Generator

    Light bulb

    Switch

15. Which of the following circuit diagrams represents a circuit that would allow the director to turn the light off and on from two different locations?

A.

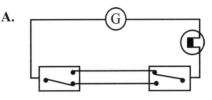

B.

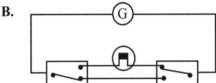

C.

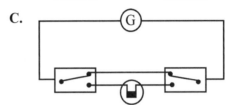

D.

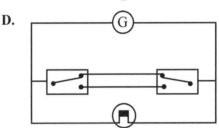

PAT, 1999

Use the following information to answer the next question.

A safety device should be inserted into the circuit illustrated in the given diagram to prevent a power surge from burning the lights out.

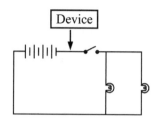

Device

16. Which device should be placed into the existing circuit?

A.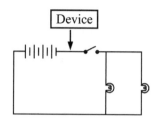

B.

C.

D.

17. Trish wants to use an electric motor to power her model car. In order to do so, Trish needs to attach a pulley to what part of the motor?

A. The electromagnet

B. The commutator

C. The armature

D. The brushes

18. A certain part consists of a metal ring split into two pieces. When the motor is in operation, this split has the function of

A. reversing the electric current through the coils in order to reverse the magnetic field polarity

B. increasing the speed of rotation of the motor by reducing electromagnetic friction

C. changing the magnetic field polarity by changing the number of coils of wire

D. decreasing the magnetic field experienced by the rotating coils

Use the following information to answer the next question.

Greg knows that the switch on a toaster is made from two different metals that expand at a different rate.

19. What type of switch does a toaster have?

A. Thermostat

B. Thermocline

C. Thermometer

D. Thermocouple

Use the following information to answer the next question.

When Jessica plugged a 1 000 W curling iron and a 1 200 W hair dryer into the same 110 V outlet, the circuit breaker tripped. She had overloaded the circuit that was rated at 12 A.

20. How many amperes of current over the safe limit were Jessica's appliances using?

A. 4

B. 6

C. 8

D. 10

Use the following information to answer the next question.

Characteristics of Cells

A. A cell converts electrical energy to chemical energy.

B. A cell consists of two different metal electrodes and an electrolyte.

C. A flashlight cell is classified as a wet cell.

D. Copper and zinc make good electrodes.

Numerical Response

1. Write the number 1 on the line above each statement that is **true**. Write the number 2 on the line above each statement that is **false**.

___ ___ ___ ___
 A   B   C   D

(Record your answer as a **four-digit** number.)

Use the following information to answer the next three questions.

The students in a science class were given a project to construct an electric car powered by a homemade battery.
They were given a set of metal electrodes and a choice of liquids to use for electrolytes. One group tested the metals to find the best pair to use. Their results are shown in the following table:

Metal	Copper	Zinc	Lead	Aluminum
Copper		1.5 V	0.8 V	0.07 V
Zinc			1.0 V	0.5 V
Lead				0.9 V

21. The **best** combination of metals to use would be

A. copper and aluminum

B. aluminum and zinc

C. zinc and copper

D. lead and zinc

22. Which of the following combinations of cells, connected in series, would **not** make a 3.0 V battery?

A. Three lead and zinc cells

B. Two copper and zinc cells

C. Six aluminum and zinc cells

D. Three aluminum and lead cells

Use the following information to answer the next question.

An electrical circuit has four basic parts.

A. Load

B. Control

C. Conductor

D. Source

The given schematic diagram represents a basic circuit.

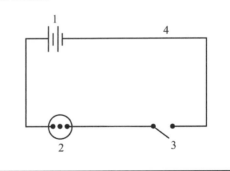

---

2. Match the basic parts of an electrical circuit to the numbered component representing that part in the diagram.
Component: ___ ___ ___ ___
Basic Part: A   B   C   D

(Record your answer as a **four-digit** number.)

Written Response

1. Explain why cogeneration is an efficient use of energy conversion.

(2 marks)

2. A container of water heated by an 800 W hot plate for 6 min gained 250 kJ of energy.

a) Calculate the heat energy used by the hot plate.

(2 marks)

b) What is the efficiency of this heating setup?

(2 marks)

ANSWERS AND SOLUTIONS—UNIT TEST

1. A	8. D	15. A	21. C
2. C	9. C	16. C	22. D
3. D	10. B	17. C	NR2. 2341
4. B	11. A	18. A	WR1. See Solution
5. D	12. C	19. A	WR2. See Solution
6. D	13. D	20. C	
7. A	14. B	NR1. 2121	

1. A

Balloon 1's overall charge is negative (6+, 7–).
Balloon 2's overall charge is negative (7+, 8–).
According to the law of electrical charges,
Balloon 1 will repel Balloon 2 because like
charges repel one another.

2. C

The law of electrical charges states that like
charges repel, and unlike charges attract.
The tumbling action in a clothes dryer produces
friction. The friction causes the electrons to leave
one sweater and accumulate on the other sweater.
The sweater that loses electrons becomes positively
charged, while the sweater that gains electrons
becomes negatively charged. Unlike charges
will attract.

3. D

The light in the room was absorbed by the solar
panel. The solar panel converted the light into
electricity. The electrical current was transmitted
by a wire to the motor. The running motor,
connected to the wheels by an elastic band,
provided the energy to make the car move.
The energy conversion was solar to electrical to
mechanical.

4. B

First, the plunger is pushed down. This is an
example of mechanical energy (energy of motion).

Pushing the plunger down causes the generator to
produce an electric current. This causes the
electricity that is produced to travel down the
wire to the explosives. This is an example of
electrical energy.

5. D

The molten rock deep inside Earth's crust heats
groundwater, changing it to steam. Iceland is able
to use this steam to heat buildings and to generate
power.

6. D

The wind turns the wind turbine. The turbine is
connected to a generator. The generator produces
electricity, which provides the current to light the
cabin. Mechanical energy is converted to electrical
energy. Electrical energy is then changed into
light energy.

7. A

Electronic devices such as MP3 players,
computers, and calculators use direct current.
The longest, thinnest wire should have the
most resistance.

8. D

Electrical resistance can be slight or great, depending on the length, thickness, and type of wire. A long, thin wire offers the most resistance.

9. C

Resistance is affected by type, length, and thickness of wire. Thick wire has less resistance than thin wire because there is a bigger path for electron flow. A short wire has less resistance than a long wire because fewer electrons are slowed down.

As thickness increases, resistance decreases, and as length increases, resistance also increases.

10. B

The amount of current used by the appliance is calculated as follows:

$$I = \frac{V}{R}$$
$$= \frac{120}{12}$$
$$= 10 \text{ A}$$

The amount of current available for another appliance is calculated as follows:
$$15 \text{ A} - 10 \text{ A} = 5 \text{ A}$$

11. A

The galvanometer works when an electrical current deflects a magnetic needle. The galvanometer measures a small current. It is connected in series into the existing circuit.

12. C

Electrical power is defined as the rate at which an electrical device converts electricity into other forms of energy. This calculation requires information about current (I) and voltage (V).
Power = Current × Voltage

13. D

$$\text{power} = \frac{\text{energy}}{\text{time}}$$
$$\text{time} = 1 \min = 60 \text{ s}$$
$$\text{energy} = \text{power} \times \text{time}$$
$$= 60 \text{ W} \times 60 \text{ m/s}$$
$$= 3\ 600 \text{ J}$$

The amount of electrical energy consumed by the bulb in 1 min is 3 600 J.

14. B

The lamps that will continue to light are the ones that have a complete circuit with no interruptions. The burnt-out L_1 and the opened S_2 are interruptions to the circuit. Therefore, lamps L_1, L_4, and L_5 will not work.

15. A

To turn a light off and on with two switches means that each switch must be able to complete or break a circuit in either of two positions. This is shown in the circuit diagram in alternative **A**. In its current position, the bulb would be off. Flipping the switch on the left up would complete the circuit, and the light bulb would light up. Flipping the second switch (right) down would break the circuit, and the bulb would go off. Flipping the first switch (left) down again would complete the circuit once again, and the bulb would light up.

16. C

A fuse (⌒⌒⌒) should be inserted. A fuse is a metallic conductor that will melt from the heat of excessive current. The fuse will interrupt the current flow before the circuit wires heat up and burn.

17. C

All the components of an electric motor (brushes, a commutator, and electromagnets) cause the armature to spin. By attaching a pulley to the armature and connecting the armature to the axle of her car, Trish would have a car that works.

18. A

As the commutator spins, it will come into contact with different brushes alternately. Since each brush has a different charge, the electric current in the wires connected to that side of the commutator will change magnetic polarity. This results in an opposite polarity force that keeps the motor spinning. At each rotation, the split disrupts the polarity and allows the magnetic field polarity to reverse.

19. A

Switches that use the differential expansion of different metals are referred to as thermostats.

20. C

$$I = \frac{P}{V}$$
$$= \frac{1\ 000\ \text{W} + 1\ 200\ \text{W}}{110\ \text{V}}$$
$$= \frac{2\ 200\ \text{W}}{110\ \text{V}}$$
$$= 20\ \text{A}$$
$$20\ \text{A} - 12\ \text{A} = 8\ \text{A}$$

NR 1   2121

A **cell,** or **battery,** converts chemical energy to electrical energy. A flashlight cell (usually a D cell) has a paste-like electrolyte and is considered to be a dry cell. Wet cells have a liquid electrolyte.

21. C

The information provided indicates that the combination of zinc and copper would result in the largest amount of energy. Zinc and copper would give a total of 1.5 V.

22. D

Use the values provided in the table to see which combination would not make a 3.0 V battery.

Two copper and zinc = 2 × 1.5 V = 3.0 V
Three lead and zinc = 3 × 1.0 V = 3.0 V
Six aluminum and zinc = 6 × 0.5 V = 3.0 V
Three aluminum and lead = 3 × 0.9 V = 2.7 V

NR 2   2341

The source of energy in an electrical circuit can be a cell, battery, or electrical outlet. The conductor, usually a wire, refers to anything that will allow electrical current to flow through. The control, or switch, turns the circuit on and off. The load is anything that converts electrical energy into other forms of energy. A load can be a light or an electrical motor.

1. *Explain why cogeneration is an efficient use of energy conversion.*

Cogeneration refers to a system that uses waste energy to produce other forms of energy. For example, burning garbage eliminates the need for a landfill and at the same time produces heat for extracting oil from the oil sands and electricity for running factories.

2. *A container of water heated by an 800 W hot plate for 6 min gained 250 kJ of energy.*

   a) *Calculate the heat energy used by the hot plate.*

$$E = P \times t$$
$$800\ \text{W} = 800\ \text{J/s}$$
$$E = 800\ \text{J/s} \times 6\ \text{min} \times 60\ \text{s/min}$$
$$E = 288\ 000\ \text{J}$$

   b) *What is the efficiency of this heating setup?*

$$\text{Efficiency} = \frac{\text{Output}}{\text{Input}} \times 100$$
$$250\ 000\ \text{J} = 250\ \text{kJ} \times 1\ 000\ \text{J/kJ}$$
$$\text{Efficiency} = \frac{250\ 000}{288\ 000} \times 100$$
$$= 86.8\%$$

NOTES

Space Exploration

SPACE EXPLORATION

Table of Correlations			
Specific Expectation	**Practice Questions**	**Unit Test Questions**	**2006 PAT**
Students will:			
E.1. Investigate and describe ways that human understanding of Earth and space has depended on technological development.			
E.1.1 identify different ideas about the nature of Earth and space based on culture and science	1, NR1	1, WR2	41
E.1.2 investigate and illustrate the contributions of technological advances—including optical telescopes, spectral analysis, and space travel—to a scientific understanding of space	2, 3	4, 6	
E.1.3 describe, in general terms, the distribution of matter in star systems, galaxies, nebulae, and the universe as a whole	NR2, NR3	2, 7	NR5
E.1.4 identify evidence for, and describe characteristics of, bodies that make up the solar system, and compare their characteristics with those of Earth	4, 5, 8	3, 5,10	44, 49
E.1.5 describe and apply techniques for determining the position and motion of objects in space including • *constructing and interpreting drawings and physical models that illustrate the motion of objects in space* • *describing in general terms how parallax and the Doppler effect are used to estimate distances of objects in space and to determine their motion* • *describing the position of objects in space using angular coordinates*	NR4, 6	9	42, 43, 45, 47, 50
E.1.6 investigate predictions about the motion, alignment, and collision of bodies in space, and critically examine the evidence on which they are based	7	12	
E.2. Identify problems in developing technologies for space exploration, describe technologies developed for life in space, and explain the scientific principles involved.			
E.2.1 analyze space environments, and identify challenges that must be met in developing life-supporting systems	9	13	
E.2.2 describe technologies for life-support systems, and interpret the scientific principles on which they are based	12	NR 2	

E.2.3 describe technologies for space transport, and interpret the scientific principles involved	13, 14, 15, 16	14, 15, 16	
E.2.4 identify materials and processes developed to meet needs in space, and identify related applications	17		
E.2.5 describe the development of artificial satellites, and explain the major purposes for which they are used	10	18	48
E.3. Describe and interpret the science of optical and radio telescopes, space probes, and remote sensing technologies.			
E.3.1 explain, in general terms, the operation of optical telescopes, including telescopes that are positioned in space environments	19, 20, 21	NR1, 20	
E.3.2 explain the role of radio and optical telescopes in determining characteristics of stars and star systems	22, 23	8	
E.3.3 describe and interpret, in general terms, the technologies used in global positioning systems and remote sensing	18	19, WR3	
E.4. Identify issues and opportunities arising from the application of space technology, identify alternatives involved, and analyze implications.			
E.4.1 recognize risks and dangers associated with space exploration	11	WR1	46
E.4.2 describe Canadian contributions to space research and development and to the astronaut program	24	17	
E.4.3 identify and analyze factors that are important to decisions regarding space exploration and development	25, 26	11	

SPACE EXPLORATION

E.1.1   identify different ideas about the nature of Earth and space based on culture and science

CULTURE AND SCIENCE

Humans have always been fascinated by entities in the sky. Many ancient tribes created stories to explain the presence and movement of objects in space. The people of the First Nations saw a distinct pattern of stars they called the Great Bear. The Egyptians built the pyramids in alignment with the seasonal position of certain stars.

Practice Questions: 1, NR1

E.1.2   investigate and illustrate the contributions of technological advances—including optical telescopes, spectral analysis, and space travel—to a scientific understanding of space

EARLY THEORIES AND TECHNOLOGICAL ADVANCES

The **geocentric** model of planetary motion was proposed by Aristotle approximately 2 000 years ago. This model has Earth at the centre with the sun, moon, and other planets orbiting it.

In the 1500s, Copernicus proposed the sun-centred, or **heliocentric model**. In this model, all the planets revolve around the sun in a concentric circular pattern.

Later, it was the work of Galileo and Kepler that determined the revolution around the sun to be an elliptical pattern.

Much of the data collected by early astronomers was gathered using simple instruments such as the quadrant, cross-staff, or astrolabe. It was, however, the invention of the telescope in the early 1600s that provided the necessary tool for studying distant objects. This invention was followed by the discovery of **spectroscopy**, the breakdown of light into its spectrum of colour. The spectrum provided information about the element composition of celestial bodies.

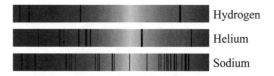

Hydrogen

Helium

Sodium

Improved optical and radio telescopes followed, and then came the age of rockets and satellites. Today, advanced computer and space technologies in the form of space stations and rovers are collecting information previously unattainable.

Scientists use the **astronomical unit** (AU) to measure distances within the solar system. The distance from the centre of Earth to the centre of the sun is 1 AU. By comparison, the distance from Mercury to the sun is 0.39 AU and from Pluto to the sun is 39.5 AU.

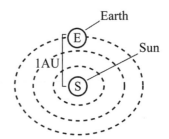

Distances beyond the solar system are measured in light-years. A **light-year** is the distance light travels in one year. After the sun, the next nearest star to Earth, Proxima Centauri, is 4.2 light-years away. The following calculation expresses the vast distance that Proxima Centauri is from Earth.

$$300\ 000 \text{ km/s} \times 60 \text{ s/min}$$
$$\times 60 \text{ min/h} \times 24 \text{ h/day}$$
$$\times 365 \text{ days/year} \times 4.2$$
$$= 3.97 \times 10^{13} \text{ km}$$

Practice Questions: 2, 3

E.1.3   describe, in general terms, the distribution of matter in star systems, galaxies, nebulae, and the universe as a whole

E.1.4   identify evidence for, and describe characteristics of, bodies that make up the solar system, and compare their characteristics with those of Earth

THE SOLAR SYSTEM

It is believed that huge accumulations of dust and gases called **nebulae** are pulled together by gravity to form stars. It appears that stars go through stages of development. They begin as red giants, become white dwarfs, and eventually evolve to supernovas and neutron stars or black holes. Scientific evidence shows they move through this progression.

The sun is the nearest star to Earth. It is the basis of the solar system that includes eight planets and their moons. All the planets revolve around the sun in an elliptical orbit and rotate on their axis to produce day and night.

The **terrestrial planets** of Mercury, Venus, Earth, and Mars are closer to the sun and are made of solid material. Jupiter, Saturn, Uranus, and Neptune are much larger but less dense. These planets are made of gases, usually hydrogen and helium and are referred to as **Jovian planets**.

The asteroid belt is found between the orbits of Jupiter and Mars. Asteroids are rocky or metallic and revolve around the sun, as do the other planets.

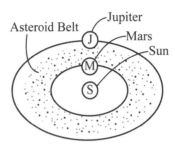

Fragments of rocks called **meteoroids** are often pulled toward Earth by gravity. As they enter the atmosphere, friction causes the rocks to heat up and shower a streak of light. These shooting stars or **meteors** frequently burn up in the atmosphere. Occasionally, a rock crashes down to Earth's surface as a **meteorite**.

Comets are also found travelling in the solar system. They are made up of dust and ice. The sun's heat causes the ice to vaporize and leave a trail of visible gases. Halley's comet orbits the sun; therefore, it has a predictable schedule and becomes visible every 76 years.

Practice Questions: NR2, NR3, 4, 5, 8

E.1.5 *describe and apply techniques for determining the position and motion of objects in space, including*

- *constructing and interpreting drawings and physical models that illustrate the motion of objects in space*
- *describing in general terms how parallax and the Doppler effect are used to estimate distances of objects in space and to determine their motion*
- *describing the position of objects in space using angular coordinates*

MEASURING DISTANCES IN SPACE

To estimate the distance of an object from Earth, astronomers use the parallax of a star. **Parallax** refers to the apparent shift in position of the star when it is viewed from different places. The speed and direction of motion of an object in space are determined based on the Doppler effect.

The **Doppler effect** is the change in frequency of a wave as it moves toward or away from an observer.

Two important measurements are used to describe the position of objects in space.

1. The **azimuth** is the direction relative to due north (0 degrees).

2. The altitude is the height in the sky of the object measured in degrees from 0 to 90. Zero degrees is at the horizon, while 90 degrees is straight up.

The location of a star is recorded as an azimuth of *x* degrees and an altitude of *y* degrees.

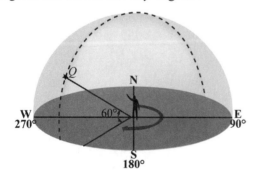

Practice Questions: NR4, 6

E.1.6 *investigate predictions about the motion, alignment, and collision of bodies in space, and critically examine the evidence on which they are based*

MOTION AND ECLIPSES

Because of the predictable pattern of Earth's revolution around the sun and the moon's revolution around Earth, the sun, Earth, and moon can align in a straight line relative to one another. This produces a shadow called an **eclipse**.

A solar eclipse occurs when the moon aligns itself between Earth and the sun.

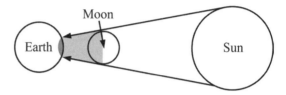

A lunar eclipse occurs when Earth aligns itself between the sun and the moon.

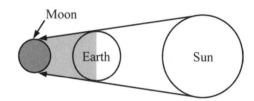

Planets, comets, asteroids, and meteoroids are in constant motion in space. Occasionally, some space matter leaves its orbit and falls to Earth. It is believed that the Barringer Crater in Arizona was formed by the impact of a meteorite that fell to Earth about 50 000 years ago. More frequent are smaller meteorite collisions with Earth. Thousands of tiny meteorites hit Earth each year.

Practice Question: 7

E.2.1   analyze space environments, and identify challenges that must be met in developing life-supporting systems

SPACE ENVIRONMENT

Space is a harsh and dangerous environment. There are many challenges that must be met in order for people to safely work and live.

There is no air or atmospheric pressure in space. There is no food or water. Everything people need to survive must be taken with them. Spacecraft must also have systems to dispose of and recycle waste safely, including human waste.

Earth's atmosphere keeps it warm and protects living things from most cosmic radiation. In space, there is no protection. It is extremely cold and has dangerous cosmic radiation and micrometeorites. The walls of a spacecraft and space suits used for space walks must be constructed of materials that can withstand these hazards.

The microgravity environment of space is also hard on the bones and muscles of astronauts. Astronauts living in space for extended periods of time must exercise intensely to overcome these effects.

Objects in space are very far apart. This means that astronauts may be in space for extended periods of time as they travel from one place to another. In the days of the Apollo missions to the moon, astronauts were in space between 8 and 12 days at a time. Currently, astronauts may be on the International Space Station for months at a time. In the future, missions to Mars will be up to two years long. This extended time means that they are exposed to the dangers of space for longer and longer durations.

Practice Question: 9

E.2.2   describe technologies for life-support systems, and interpret the scientific principles on which they are based

LIFE-SUPPORT SYSTEMS IN SPACE

The International Space Station (ISS) has a number of different life-support systems. These systems are designed to meet the challenges of living and working in space.

Oxygen is both shipped to the ISS in pressurized tanks and created onboard using recycled water. The oxygen and hydrogen are separated using a process called electrolysis. As a backup, there is a system called a perchlorate candle that produces oxygen through a chemical reaction.

Recycled wastewater is used to produce drinking water. The system for purifying the water on the space station mimics the natural water cycle on Earth.

Scientists are also experimenting with growing food in space. This will be necessary for long manned flights such as missions to Mars where it will be impossible to take all the food they would need for the entire journey. They are experimenting with hydroponic systems where plants grow in a liquid environment. These plants may also one day provide not only food, but a system to produce oxygen and remove carbon dioxide from the air, just as they do on Earth.

Practice Question: 12

E.2.3 *describe technologies for space transport, and interpret the scientific principles involved*

SPACE TRANSPORT

The main types of space transport are rockets, space shuttles space stations, and space probes.

ROCKETS

A rocket is a transport vehicle that carries astronauts and satellites into space. To overcome the force of gravity, an object needs to be travelling at least 28 000 km/h. Burning solid fuels such as oxygen and nitrogen creates the propulsion required. The gas is compressed and pushed out through the boosters. This causes a reaction that moves the rocket forward.

The power of rockets to lift objects into space is described by **Newton's third law of motion**, which states that every action causes an equal and opposite reaction.

The motion of satellites and interplanetary spacecraft in space is described by the laws of motion formulated by Kepler, which state that the closer a satellite is to Earth, the faster it orbits.

Multistage rockets consist of two or more sections called **stages**. In multistage rockets, each stage is separated and discarded once its fuel has been consumed. Successively discarding the stages reduces the weight of the fuselage and increases the mass ratio of the rocket. This is an efficient method of increasing the speed of the rocket.

A rocket consists of three main parts:

• Payload—crew and cargo

• Fuel—combination of gases

• Mechanical structure—combustion chamber and tanks

SPACE SHUTTLES, SPACE STATIONS, AND SPACE PROBES

There are three main types of spacecraft in use: space shuttles, space stations, and space probes.

The **space shuttle** is a reusable rocket-launched vehicle designed to go into Earth's orbit, transport people and cargo between Earth and orbiting spacecrafts, and glide to a landing back on Earth. Space shuttles have been used to service and repair orbiting satellites, to return previously deployed spacecrafts, and to conduct scientific experiments in space.

Space stations are facilities that enable humans to live in space for long periods of time.

Space stations are used as laboratories where scientific and engineering experiments can be conducted. One day, they will be used as servicing centres where spacecrafts can be repaired, upgraded, or even constructed, and as spaceports where spacecrafts can pick up and deliver people, cargo, and fuel on the way to or returning from distant destinations.

Space probes are unmanned satellites or remote-controlled landing devices that explore objects and areas in space. Space probes have been used to carry out remote sensing on Mercury and Jupiter. They have been used to collect samples of soil on Mars, to collect data on Venus, and study the nature of Saturn's rings.

Practice Questions: 13, 14, 15, 16

E.2.4 *identify materials and processes developed to meet needs in space, and identify related applications*

TECHNOLOGY NEEDS IN SPACE AND THEIR SPINOFFS

Space exploration requires specialized mechanical, computer, communications, and medical technology. There are many technologies that people use in their day-to-day activities that are spinoffs from the technologies used in space exploration.

- Specialized computer chips used for images in the Hubble Space Telescope are used for digital imaging in diagnosing medical conditions, such as some types of cancer.

- Air monitoring equipment for space is used to check for industrial pollution emissions.

- Water purification systems used for recovering and purifying water in space are used as commercial and residential purifiers.

- Food preservation and packing techniques for meeting needs in space are used for emergency reserves on Earth.

- Structural analysis equipment used to detect structural defects in spacecraft is now used in the automobile industry for checking welding joints.

- Robots for repair and assembly in space are used in the automobile industry for the assembly of parts.

- Wireless communication technology developed for space is now used in GPS technology on Earth.

- Protective material for space suits is being used for firefighters' suits.

Practice Question: 17

E.2.5 *describe the development of artificial satellites, and explain the major purposes for which they are used*

ARTIFICIAL SATELLITES

Any object purposely placed in Earth's orbit or in orbit around other planets is called an **artificial satellite**. The first artificial satellite was launched in 1957. Since then, thousands of satellites have been rocketed into Earth's orbit. Artificial satellites play an important role in communication, military intelligence, and scientific studies.

The telecommunication industry uses communications satellites to carry radio, television, and telephone signals. Navigational satellites point out locations of objects on Earth, while weather satellites help meteorological departments forecast the weather. Satellites can also be used for research purposes. Landsat and RADARSAT, two Canadian satellites, have been used for activities such as monitoring environmental changes, tracking forest fires, and even monitoring soil quality.

Practice Questions: 10

E.3.1 *explain, in general terms, the operation of optical telescopes, including telescopes that are positioned in space environments*

OPTICAL TELESCOPES

A telescope is a device that allows distant objects to be seen as if they are much closer and brighter. Telescopes are used to observe celestial objects.

Most telescopes work by collecting and magnifying the visible light that is given off by stars or reflected from the surface of planets. These telescopes use light and are called **optical telescopes**. There are two main types of optical telescopes: refracting and reflecting telescopes.

Refracting telescopes use convex lenses to collect light from a distant object and focus it so it can be seen clearly. The first telescope ever invented was a refracting telescope.

Reflecting telescopes use curved mirrors to bring reflected light waves to a focal point in order to view distant objects.

Optical interferometry is a technique that uses several telescopes to improve the resolution of images. In this technique, signals from telescopes in separate locations are combined. Optical interferometers are useful for making relatively bright, closely paired objects visible.

The **Hubble Space Telescope** (HST) is named after American astronomer Edwin P. Hubble. It was launched on April 24, 1990, and orbits about 600 km above Earth. In the Hubble telescope, a series of mirrors are used to focus light from very distant objects. The telescope is 4.3 m in diameter and 13 m in length. In July 1994, HST provided astronomers with the first convincing evidence of the existence of black holes. It also provided amazing images of Jupiter when the comet Shoemaker Levy 9 impacted the planet in July 1994. These images have helped scientists obtain data for spectral analysis of Jupiter's atmosphere.

Practice Questions: 19, 20, 21

E.3.2   explain the role of radio and optical telescopes in determining characteristics of stars and star systems

RADIO TELESCOPES

A **radio telescope** consists of a radio receiver and an antenna system that is used to detect radio frequency radiation. Radio wavelengths are longer than those of visible light, so radio telescopes have to be very large to attain the resolution of optical telescopes.

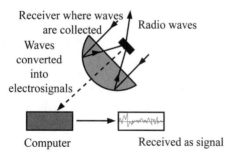

An advantage of radio telescopes is that they use radio waves and not visible light waves. Radio waves are not as easily distorted as light waves, and they are detectable at any time of day. Radio waves can detect objects that do not emit visible light. These telescopes can also be combined in **radio interferometry** to produce high resolution images. A group of many telescopes is called an **array**.

Optical and radio telescopes provide information about the objects in space.

Practice Questions: 22, 23

E.3.3   describe and interpret, in general terms, the technologies used in global positioning systems and remote sensing

SATELLITE TECHNOLOGIES

The **Global Positioning System** (GPS) is a space-based navigation system. It consists of 24 satellites that are orbiting Earth. At any point in time, three satellites are above a certain area and can relay information about the relative position of a receiver on Earth. Information collected from the three satellites is processed using triangulation.

Remote sensing is another technology involving satellites. Satellites orbiting relatively near Earth use sensors to measure the amount of energy, reflected from Earth's surface. This data provides information about the environment and can show changes that occurred on Earth's surface.

Practice Questions: 18

E.4.1 recognize risks and dangers associated with space exploration

RISKS AND DANGERS ASSOCIATED WITH SPACE EXPLORATION

There are many risks and dangers associated with space exploration. In space, there is no air, no food, and no water. Furthermore, there are deadly hazards such as solar and cosmic radiation, micrometeorites, and extreme temperatures.

Accidents related to space travel result in huge economic loss and often the loss of human life. In February 2003, the space shuttle *Columbia* sustained damage to the heat-resistant tiles on the underside of the craft. When it re-entered Earth's atmosphere, it exploded and burned up over Texas. The entire seven-member crew perished.

Practice Question: 11

E.4.2 describe Canadian contributions to space research and development and to the astronaut program

CANADIAN CONTRIBUTIONS TO SPACE EXPLORATION

Canada's involvement with the space program started in 1962 with the launch of the satellite Alouette 1.

In 1972, Canada launched its first communications satellite Anik. The RADARSAT and Landsat satellites were later launched for the purposes of monitoring environmental changes on Earth's surface. Perhaps Canada's greatest contribution to the program has been the design and construction of the robot arms Canadarm 1 and Canadarm 2. Canadarm 1 was designed for the space shuttle and has been used to repair the Hubble Space Telescope. Canadarm 2 has been used for constructing the International Space Station. Canada was also responsible for making the ramp used during the Mars Pathfinder mission.

Some famous Canadian astronauts include Marc Garneau, who was the first Canadian in space, and more recently, Chris Hadfield, who became the first Canadian to walk in space in 2001.

Practice Question: 24

E.4.3 identify and analyze factors that are important to decisions regarding space exploration and development

SPACE EXPLORATION ISSUES AND CONCERNS

Space exploration helps to ensure that humanity can continue to grow and expand even beyond what the natural world here on Earth can provide. At some point in the future, Earth alone may not be able to provide sufficient resources to sustain life. Space contains many mineral resources such as gold, iron, and platinum that could be used. Scientists are also looking for ways of capturing solar energy in space and redirecting it to Earth.

The quest to explore space has led to many great technologies. Medical imaging, bar coding, vision screening, ear thermometers, cordless tools, lithium batteries, and robotic arms are some of the technologies developed from the space program. These technologies are used on Earth for the benefit of humankind. Global positioning systems, remote-sensing, weather forecasting, and satellite communication have opened a great avenue for future development.

Since space contains so many valuable resources, questions arise concerning the ownership of space and what countries these resources belong to. An ethical concern about space exploration is the money spent when worldwide poverty exists.

Environmentalists discuss the topic of protecting space from unnecessary alteration and who will ultimately be responsible for cleaning up space junk and pollution.

Practice Questions: 25, 26

PRACTICE QUESTIONS—SPACE EXPLORATION

1. Throughout time, people have created stories and proposed theories about space. The Aboriginal people are known for their legends that dealt with
   A. predictions of comets
   B. descriptions of planets
   C. explanations of space travel
   D. formations of star constellations

Use the following information to answer the next question.

Four scientists and their contributions to the study of space are listed below.

1. Kepler proposed that the planets revolve around the sun in an elliptical orbit.

2. Aristotle proposed that Earth is in the centre and all the planets revolve around Earth.

3. Galileo used the telescope to confirm the sun-centred model of planetary movement.

4. Copernicus proposed the heliocentric model of planetary motion.

Numerical Response

1. Listed from the earliest contribution to the most recent contribution, the order is
____, ____, ____, and ____. (Record your answer as a **four-digit** number.)

Use the following information to answer the next question.

Proxima Centauri, the star closest to Earth other than the sun, is moving away from Earth.

Astronomers know that Alpha Centauri is moving away from Earth because the wavelength of its light is becoming _**i**_ and the colour band for its light is shifting to the _**ii**_ end of the spectrum.

2. The given statement is completed by the information in row

Row	*i*	*ii*
A.	stretched out	blue
B.	stretched out	red
C.	compressed	blue
D.	compressed	red

3. The Hubble has provided an important contribution to the study of space. It has given information about galaxies, black holes, and supernovas. The Hubble is a
   A. satellite telescope
   B. space shuttle
   C. space probe
   D. rocket

Use the following information to answer the next question.

A star is a burning ball of gases that has different stages in its life cycle. Four of these stages are given below.

   1. Neutron star   2. Nebulae

   3. Supernova   4. Red giant

Numerical Response

2. Listed in order from the first stage in a star's life cycle to the last stage, the stages are
____, ____, ____, and ____. (Record your answer as a **four-digit** number.)

Use the following information to answer the next question.

I. A formation of stars is called a constellation.

II. Stars start out as an accumulation of dust and gases called a nebula.

III. The Milky Way is another name for an exploding star.

IV. Galaxies can be classified as spiral, elliptical, or irregular.

Numerical Response

3. Place the number 1 in the blank if the corresponding statement is true and the number 2 if it is false.

____ ____ ____ ____
 I   II   III   IV

(Record your answer as a **four-digit** number.)

Use the following information to answer the next question.

Students in a Grade 9 science class were asked to imagine that a new planet, *W*, has been discovered and its location has to be determined given certain characteristics.

Planet	Radius (Earth = 1)	Density (Earth = 1)	Surface Material	Atmosphere
Venus	0.95	0.86	Thin rocky crust	Carbon dioxide
Earth	1	1	Rocky mantle/ water	Nitrogen/ oxygen
Jupiter	11.25	0.24	Gaseous	Hydrogen/ helium
Saturn	9.45	0.13	Gaseous	Hydrogen/ helium
Planet W	0.89	0.76	Rocky crust	Carbon dioxide

---

4. Given this information, it can be hypothesized that planet *W* would be located between

A. Venus and Earth

B. Earth and Jupiter

C. Jupiter and Saturn

D. Saturn and Neptune

5. Venus is farther away from the sun than Mercury. However, Venus has a much higher average surface temperature (480°C) compared with that of Mercury (180°C). The reason for this difference is that Venus

A. is a larger planet than Mercury

B. is made up of a red, rocky material

C. has a thick atmosphere of carbon dioxide gas

D. spins more slowly on its axis than Mercury

Use the following information to answer the next question.

Calvin is setting up a model of the solar system. He positions a cardboard sun at one end of a school hallway and Pluto at the other end, 20 m away. Calvin knows that Pluto is 39.5 AU (astronomical units) from the sun and Jupiter is 5.27 AU from the sun.

Numerical Response

4. In order to make his model to scale, how many metres from the cardboard sun should Calvin place Jupiter? _____ m.
(Record your answer to **two** decimal places.)

Copyright Protected

6. The terms azimuth and altitude are associated with determining the

   A. distance to the stars and planets

   B. location of the stars and planets

   C. brightness of the stars and planets

   D. composition of the stars and planets

7. A total solar eclipse was observed across the Antarctic on November 23, 2003. This meant that the sun, Earth, and moon were in what alignment?

   A. The sun was between Earth and the moon.

   B. The moon was between the sun and Earth.

   C. Earth was between the moon and the sun.

   D. Earth was between the moon and the sun, but the moon was lower and the sun was higher.

8. Small bodies orbiting around a planet are called

   A. asteroids

   B. satellites

   C. galaxies

   D. nebulae

9. Which of the following issues is **not** a challenge in sustaining a safe and healthy environment aboard a spacecraft?

   A. Cosmic radiation

   B. Waste management

   C. Overcoming gravity

   D. Maintaining atmosphere

10. Russia became the first country to launch an artificial satellite in 1957. This satellite was called

   A. Luna

   B. Soyuz

   C. Sputnik

   D. Alouette

Use the following information to answer the next question.

Russian cosmonaut Valeri Polyakov completed a 438-day tour of duty aboard the Mir Space Station in 1995.

11. Which of the following aspects of living in space would have been the **least** hazardous for him?

   A. Lower food consumption

   B. Environmental dangers

   C. Psychological issues

   D. Microgravity

Use the following information to answer the next question.

Air, water, and other wastes are recycled aboard the International Space Station (ISS). Oxygen is carried in liquid form.

12. The **main** reason that the ISS has adopted the given strategies is to overcome

   A. the excessive cost of living in space

   B. issues related to onboard experiments

   C. the scarcity of resources on a space station

   D. the lack of storage space aboard a space station

13. A scientific law that explains why rockets are able to lift objects into space was first developed by

   A. Pascal

   B. Kepler

   C. Newton

   D. Rutherford

14. The payload of a spacecraft refers to the
   A. materials carried aboard
   B. combustion chamber
   C. launching pad
   D. rocket fuel

15. NASA, the Soviet Space Program, the European Space Agency, and some other participating countries set up a permanent space station called
   A. Freedom
   B. Skylab
   C. Mir
   D. ISS

16. Unmanned vehicles launched into space in order to carry out remote sensing and collect data are called
   A. space probes
   B. space shuttles
   C. space stations
   D. space laboratories

17. The technology for improving the traction of car tires is adapted from the space technology developed for
   A. advanced parachute material
   B. structural analysis of spacecraft
   C. analysis of rocket engine emissions
   D. microcircuitry designs for electronics

Use the following information to answer the next question.

The United States Air Force operates a system called NAVSTAR, which is a global positioning system (GPS) that consists of 24 satellites.

18. To find the position of any object on Earth, the GPS uses signals from
   A. six out of 24 satellites
   B. two out of 24 satellites
   C. five out of 24 satellites
   D. three out of 24 satellites

19. Telescopes in which lenses are used to bend light and bring it images into focus are called
   A. refracting telescopes
   B. reflecting telescopes
   C. radiation telescopes
   D. glass telescopes

20. Reflecting telescopes collect light by using a combination of
   A. convex lenses
   B. concave lenses
   C. convex mirrors
   D. concave mirrors

21. Astronomers use computers to correct the image distortion caused by Earth's atmosphere on the quality of images gathered by telescopes. This technique is known as
   A. refractive optics
   B. reflective optics
   C. adaptive optics
   D. binary optics

22. Radio telescopes have a larger dish than optical telescopes because radio waves
   A. travel at a higher speed
   B. travel a greater distance
   C. are easily distorted by atmosphere.
   D. have a longer wavelength than that of visible light

23. Which of the following statements about radio waves is **false**?

   A. Radio waves are unaffected by clouds, pollution, and atmospheric disturbances.

   B. Radio telescopes are used to study objects in space.

   C. Radio waves cannot be detected during the day.

   D. Radio waves can be detected at night.

Use the following information to answer the next question.

Since its maiden voyage aboard the space shuttle Columbia in 1981, the Canadarm I has demonstrated its reliability. It is one of Canada's major contributions to the field of space exploration.

24. The Canadarm I has been used on the Hubble Space Telescope as a

   A. landing pad

   B. repairing tool

   C. stabilizer

   D. launcher

Use the following information to answer the next question.

Marla writes these statements about the International Space Station (ISS).

1. The ISS is solely an American project.

2. The ISS is powered by the sun's energy.

3. The ISS is a research facility.

4. The ISS orbits around Earth.

25. Which of the given statements describing the ISS is incorrect?

   A. Statement 1

   B. Statement 2

   C. Statement 3

   D. Statement 4

Use the following information to answer the next question.

Shelley was given a list of facts related to space exploration and was assigned the task of grouping them into the positive and negative aspects of space research.

1. Space exploration is dangerous and poses a risk to human life.

2. Space exploration has resulted in a more efficient method of communication.

3. Space exploration is a possible source of future resources.

4. Space exploration could provide a place to live.

5. Space exploration is a very costly venture.

26. The facts that Shelley would **most likely** classify as positive aspects for space exploration are facts

   A. 1, 2, and 3

   B. 2, 4, and 5

   C. 1, 2, and 5

   D. 2, 3, and 4

ANSWERS AND SOLUTIONS—PRACTICE QUESTIONS

1. D	4. A	9. C	15. D	21. C
NR1. 2413	5. C	10. C	16. A	22. D
2. B	NR4. 2.67	11. A	17. A	23. C
3. A	6. B	12. D	18. D	24. B
NR2. 2431	7. B	13. C	19. A	25. A
NR3. 1121	8. B	14. A	20. D	26. D

1. D

The aboriginal people looked into the skies and saw star formations. For example, they saw the constellation Ursa Major as a bear running away from hunters.

NR 1   2413

Aristotle (320 BC) proposed that Earth was the centre of all activity. According to him, the sun, moon, and all visible planets revolved around Earth. Copernicus (1543) proposed that the sun was the centre of all planetary movement and all planets revolved in concentric circles. Kepler (1609) said that the movement of the planets was in an elliptical pattern rather than in concentric circles. With the aid of the telescope, Galileo (1615) confirmed planetary motion around the sun.

2. B

Scientists can tell that Alpha Centauri is moving away from Earth because the wavelength of its light is becoming stretched out and the colour band for its light is shifting to the red end of the spectrum. This redshift of the colour band occurs when a light source moves away from an observer.

3. A

The Hubble, sometimes called HST (Hubble Space Telescope), was first launched in 1990. HST has sent to Earth well over 100 000 pictures of nebulae, galaxies, planets, black holes, and fragments of the comet Shoemaker colliding with Jupiter.

NR 2   2431

A star is an accumulation of dust and gases that starts out as a nebula. As more material is drawn into the spinning nebula, temperatures reach nearly 10 000 000° C, changing hydrogen gas to helium gas. Eventually, the hydrogen gets used up and further nuclear reactions cause the expansion of the outer layers. The star becomes a red giant. Eventually, the nuclear reaction stops. This causes the star to shrink into a dwarf. When the star runs out of fuel, gravity causes the star to collapse. An explosion occurs and a supernova is born. If a core still remains, the intense gravity causes a neutron star or black hole to form.

NR 3   1121

Some 88 different groupings of stars or constellations have been identified. Orion, the Hunter, is one of them. Stars start out as an accumulation of gases and dust drawn together by gravity to form nebulae. Groupings of billions of stars held together by gravity are often called galaxies. Galaxies can appear spiral, elliptical, or irregular. The spiral galaxy that Earth is located in is the Milky Way.

4. A

The so-called terrestrial planets near the sun are composed of a more dense solid material. The larger Jovian planets are composed of a less dense gaseous material and are distant from the sun. Because Planet W is small (radius 0.95) and relatively dense (0.76) one can assume that it would belong to the inner terrestrial planets. Therefore, Planet W would orbit between Venus and Earth.

5. C

Venus has an atmosphere of carbon dioxide gas. Carbon dioxide has the ability to trap the sun's heat. This is known as the greenhouse effect.

NR 4   2.67

Pluto: 39.5 AU → 20 m
Jupiter: 5.27 AU → d

Set up a ratio and cross-multiply.
$39.5d = 5.27 \times 20$
$$d = \frac{5.27 \times 20}{39.5}$$
$$= 2.668 \text{ or } 2.67 \text{ (two decimal places)}$$

Jupiter should be placed 2.67 m from the sun.

6. B

Azimuth is a compass reading relative to north. It can be a reading up to 360° horizontally. Altitude is the measure of a celestial body above the horizon. Its reading can be an angle up to 90°. Together, the azimuth and the altitude determine the location of distant objects such as stars.

7. B

A total eclipse occurs when the moon is in direct alignment between the sun and Earth. The result is a total blockage of the sun with the exception of the outer fringe.

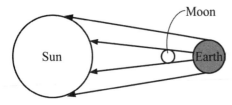

8. B

Small bodies orbiting around large bodies in space are called satellites. The moon revolves around Earth; hence, the moon is called a satellite of Earth. The moon is a natural satellite. Artificial satellites have been launched into space for various purposes and revolve around Earth. Asteroids are space rocks. Nebulae are the birthplace of stars. The sun, moon, and the eight planets of the solar system belong to a galaxy called the Milky Way.

9. C

Overcoming gravity is a challenge to get into space. But once there, waste management, maintaining atmosphere, and cosmic radiation are challenges to the environment of the spacecraft.

10. C

Russia became the first country to launch an artificial satellite in 1957. It was called Sputnik, which is the Russian word for satellite. It was only about as large as a basketball.

11. A

Lower food consumption is not a major concern while living in space. Some major concerns are the fact that space has no atmosphere, no air to breathe, no water to drink, and zero gravity. There are also many small celestial bodies such as meteorites that may hit the spacecraft. The crew members have to spend every minute of every day in a small chamber with the same people for long periods. This may lead to psychological problems. Exposure to microgravity has physical effects on the human body.

12. D

The main reason for adopting these strategies is the lack of storage space aboard the space station. An average human needs approximately 3.5 kg of oxygen, food, and water per day. If these items were carried to space in their original form, they would occupy too much space and weigh too much.

13. C

Sir Isaac Newton stated three laws of motion. Rocket liftoff is based on the third law of motion, which states that every action has an equal and opposite reaction.

14. A

Payload refers to the materials carried during a flight including crew, food, water, and air.

15. D

The International Space Station (ISS) is a joint venture of NASA, the Soviet Space Program, the European Space Agency, and other countries.

Skylab was a space station launched in 1973, and Freedom was a space station launched in 1984. These two space stations were the achievements of NASA. Russia launched Mir space station in 1994. The projects of the Freedom and Mir space stations were combined to set up ISS permanently in space. Canada provided a robotic arm and a service centre. The work started in 1998. The first crew consisting of an American and two Russians arrived there in November 2000.

16. A

Space probes such as Ranger, Mariner, Global Explorer (2000), and Mars Pathfinder (2004) were unmanned vehicle launched into space to carry out remote sensing and collect data. These probes were able to carry equipment to planets where humans cannot yet reach.

17. A

The technology for improving the traction of car tires is adapted from the space technology that arose from the development of parachute material for the Viking space mission.

18. D

There are 24 GPS satellites orbiting Earth at all times. The GPS system uses signals from three out of 24 satellites at any one time. The global positioning system is a space-based navigation system. Receivers pick up the GPS satellite signals, which are translated into a message by a computer in the receiver.

19. A

In refracting telescopes, the lenses are used to bend (refract) light and bring it into focus. Reflecting telescopes use a mirror and a lens to collect and focus light. Radiation telescopes capture images outside of the visible spectrum, and in glass telescopes, light passes directly through the glass without being altered.

20. D

Reflecting telescopes use a combination of concave mirrors to collect light. The light is then focused into an eyepiece using a concave lens.

21. C

Astronomers have used computers to develop a technique known as adaptive optics to improve the quality of images gathered by telescopes. The adaptive optic technology analyzes the blurring created by the atmosphere and compensates for the distortion, creating sharper images.

22. D

Radio telescopes must be larger than optical telescopes because radio waves have a longer wavelength compared to that of visible light. Electromagnetic waves of light have a wavelength of about 1 micrometre (0.001), but radio waves are between 1 m to 1 km in length. It requires a larger dish to collect the longer waves.

23. C

Radio waves can be detected during the day as well as at night. Even faint radio signals can be detected around the clock. Radio telescopes have advantages over optical telescopes because radio waves have a long wavelength and are unaffected by clouds and pollution.

24. B

The Canadarm I space shutter was used to make repairs on the Hubble Space Telescope.

25. A

The ISS is a joint venture of 16 countries. It is a research facility that orbits Earth. The ISS is powered by photovoltaic cells that use the sun's energy.

26. D

These are some positive aspects of space exploration:

1. Development of the satellite system used for communication.

2. Iron in asteroids and meteors that could possibly be tapped into when supplies on Earth are depleted.

3. Space stations that could serve as human habitats when extreme overcrowding takes place on Earth.

UNIT TEST—SPACE EXPLORATION

1. Ursa Major (Great Bear) is the name that was given to a

   A. comet

   B. planet

   C. satellite

   D. constellation

Use the following information to answer the next question.

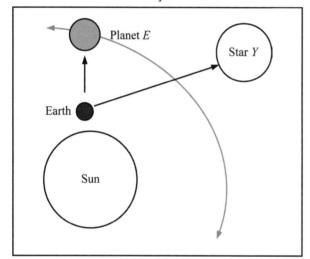

2. The distances between Planet *E* and Earth and Star *Y* and Earth can **best** be measured in

   A. light-years for both distances

   B. astronomical units for both distances

   C. astronomical units for planet *E* and light-years for star *Y*

   D. light-years for planet *E* and astronomical units for star *Y*

3. Which of the following statements about the solar system is **true**?

   A. Jupiter is larger and closer to the sun than Earth.

   B. Venus is larger and closer to the sun than Earth.

   C. Saturn is smaller and farther from the sun than Earth.

   D. Mars is smaller and farther from the sun than Earth.

Use the following information to answer the next question.

Amy was given this list of notes on early theories of celestial bodies (sun, moon, and planets).

   A. Earth centred
   B. Sun centred
   C. Proposed in the 1500s
   D. Proposed 2 000 years ago
   E. Proposed by Aristotle
   F. Proposed by Copernicus

4. The notes that are related to the heliocentric model of planetary motion are labelled

   A. A, C, and F

   B. B, C, and F

   C. A, D, and E

   D. B, C, and E

Use the following information to answer the next question.

To their surprise, a New Zealand family found that some space rock had fallen through the roof of their house and landed in the living room. The rock started out in space as a __*i*__ and ended up on Earth as a __*ii*__ .

5. This statement is completed by the information in row

Row	*i*	*ii*
A.	meteor	meteorite
B.	meteoroid	meteor
C.	meteoroid	meteorite
D.	meteorite	meteor

Use the following information to answer the next question.

Using the results of spectroscopy, an astronomer is able to determine a star's composition and its direction of movement.

6. The star corresponding to this spectrogram appears to be moving __*i*__ Earth. This shift is called the __*ii*__ effect.

The given statement is completed by the information in row

Row	*i*	*ii*
A.	toward	Kepler
B.	toward	Doppler
C.	away from	Kepler
D.	away from	Doppler

Use the following information to answer the next question.

Four characteristics of a certain type of star follow:

• Contains extremely high-density material

• Has a strong gravitational pull

• Light cannot escape from its pull of gravity

• Is difficult to detect

7. The type of star that these characteristics describe is a
   A. nebula
   B. black hole
   C. supernova
   D. white dwarf

8. By combining the information from two telescopes 100 m apart, astronomers can improve the accuracy of the images. This technique is called
   A. triangulation
   B. spectroscopy
   C. interferometry
   D. electromagnetic induction

Use the following diagram to answer the next question.

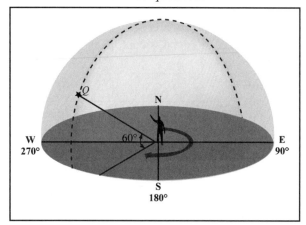

9. Which of the following rows identifies the altitude and azimuth of star *Q* relative to the position of the observer?

Row	Altitude (degrees)	Azimuth (degrees)
A.	30	80
B.	60	210
C.	80	30
D.	80	60

10. The second largest planet with rings in the solar system is

   A. Neptune

   B. Uranus

   C. Jupiter

   D. Saturn

11. Valuable natural resources such as gold and iron are known to exist in space. They are **most likely** to be found

   A. in the asteroid belt

   B. on the moon

   C. on Jupiter

   D. on Mars

12. Jen read in an astronomy book that Earth passes through the Leonid stream every 33 years, resulting in a shower of shooting stars visible on Earth. This shower is actually

   A. the tail end of a comet

   B. a cluster of brightly lit stars

   C. an explosion of a supernova

   D. many meteors entering the atmosphere

Use the following information to answer the next question.

As a result of zero gravity, crewmembers aboard spacecraft experience weightlessness.

13. Weightlessness causes physical complications that may include all of the following conditions **except**

   A. anemia

   B. blocked sinuses

   C. extra weight gain

   D. loss of bone tissue

Use the following information to answer the next question.

The most powerful rocket is the Energia multistage rocket, which was used by the Soviet Space Shuttle. In multistage rockets, each stage is separated and discarded once its fuel has been consumed.

14. This successive discarding of stages is done in order to

   A. reduce the weight of the fuselage

   B. minimize the risk of malfunctions

   C. decrease the speed of the rocket

   D. reduce the cost of launching

15. While ion drives are engines that use xenon gas instead of chemical fuels, solar sails use

A. energy of the wind

B. heat energy of the sun

C. electromagnetic energy of the sun

D. recycled energy of conventional hydrocarbon fuels

16. Space shuttles are used for deploying satellites into orbit, carrying out scientific experiments, and repairing orbiting satellites. Which of the following functions is also a function of a space shuttle?

A. Returning previously deployed satellites to Earth

B. Forecasting weather conditions

C. Taking photographs in space

D. Observing celestial bodies

17. Satellites are used to follow ships at sea, monitor soil quality, track forest fires, and search for natural resources. The name of one of these Canadian satellites is

A. Telestar   B. Landsat

C. TIROS   D. GOES

Use the following information to answer the next question.

NASA launched the first telephone and television satellite in 1962. The United States Department of Defence launched Syncom 3 in 1964.

18. In order to receive continuous signals for television communication and direct broadcast, a satellite is placed in a

A. high orbit around Earth

B. low orbit around Earth

C. geostationary orbit

D. synchronous orbit

19. The Hubble Space Telescope has provided the best available information about

A. life on the moon

B. the rings around Saturn

C. the presence of useful natural resources on the moon

D. the collision of Jupiter and the comet Shoemaker Levy 9

Use the following information to answer the next two questions.

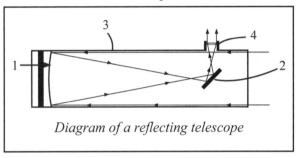

Diagram of a reflecting telescope

20. A technique that uses several telescopes linked together to produce an image with a sharper resolution is called

A. an array

B. magnification

C. interferometry

D. remote sensing

Numerical Response

1. Match each numbered structure on the diagram of the reflecting telescope with its corresponding name.

___   ___   ___   ___

Eyepiece   Secondary mirror   Primary mirror   Body tube

(Record your answer as a **four-digit** number.)

Use the following information to answer the next question.

Space exploration is making use of new technologies. Here are four statements about recent technological advancements:

1. Cost-effective xenon gas is used as rocket fuel.

2. Sunlight is harnessed to propel space vehicles.

3. Spacecraft can carry out robotic exploration.

4. Orbiting space communities now exist.

Numerical Response

2. Match each statement above with the technology that relates to it, as given below.

_____ _____ _____ _____

Solar   Ion drive   Space   Space
sail   probe   station

(Record your answer as a **four-digit** number.)

Written Response

1. List four hazards associated with survival in space.

(2 marks)

2. Compare the heliocentric and geocentric models of the solar system.

	Heliocentric Model	**Geocentric Model**
Who proposed the model?		
What was proposed?		

(2 marks)

3. A car is stuck in a remote rural area, but luckily it has a GPS system. Explain what GPS is and how it works to locate the stranded vehicle.

(2 marks)

ANSWERS AND SOLUTIONS—UNIT TEST

1. D	6. D	11. A	16. A	NR1. 4213
2. C	7. B	12. D	17. B	NR2. 2134
3. D	8. C	13. C	18. C	WR1. See Solution
4. B	9. B	14. A	19. D	WR2. See Solution
5. C	10. D	15. C	20. C	WR3. See Solution

1. D

Ancient people created stories to explain star formations. The Aboriginal people pictured the constellation Ursa Major as a bear running away from hunters.

2. C

Astronomical units are used to measure local distances such as those within the solar system. Light-years are used to measure distances beyond the solar system. Therefore, astronomical units are used for Planet *E*, and light-year units for Star *Y*.

3. D

The order of the planets from the sun is Mercury, Venus, Earth, Mars, Jupiter, Saturn, Uranus, and Neptune.

The size of planets in order from smallest to largest is Mercury, Mars, Venus, Earth, Neptune, Uranus, Saturn, and Jupiter.

Therefore, Mars is smaller and farther from the sun than Earth.

4. B

In the mid-1500s, Copernicus proposed that the sun was the centre of all activity and that all planets revolved around the sun. These notes relate to the sun-centred model that is called the heliocentric model of planetary motion.

5. C

Space debris called meteoroids become meteors as they enter Earth's atmosphere. Friction upon entry causes the meteor to burn up and shower sparks as a shooting star. If pieces land on Earth, they are called meteorites.

6. D

A star's spectrum indicates which elements are present in that star. If the star is moving away from the sun the light waves seem stretched and the spectrum has a red-shift. If the star is moving toward the sun the light waves seems squished and the spectrum has a blue-shift. This phenomenon is called the Doppler effect.

7. B

A black hole is an extremely dense remnant of a dying star. It is held together by a powerful gravitation force that does not allow light to escape. Black holes are invisible to telescopes. Astronomers know of black holes indirectly because the material near a black hole is hot and bright.

8. C

This technique is called optical interferometry. By using the Keck I and Keck II reflecting telescopes together on Mauna Kea in Hawaii, scientists are able to span greater distances and come up with clearer images of celestial bodies.

9. B

Altitude represents the height above the observer, which in this case is 60°. The azimuth is the horizontal reading starting from north and rotating 360°. In this case, the angle is 30° past south or $180° + 30° = 210°$.

10. D

Jupiter is the largest planet with three thin rings. Saturn is the second largest planet with over a thousand distinctive rings.

11. A

Outer space can be a potential source for natural resources. An asteroid belt lies between Mars and Jupiter and contains rocky chunks floating in space. These rocks contain iron, gold, and platinum. Mars and Jupiter are still relatively unexplored and cannot be listed as sources for natural resources. Recent analysis has shown that a large portion of the moon's surface is covered by silicon, aluminum, and magnesium, which are less valuable natural resources than gold and iron.

12. D

The Leonid stream is a stream of meteoroids left behind by the dust trail of the temple-tuttle comet. Earth passes through this stream every fall. Due to friction with the atmosphere, they become visible and the effect is known as a meteor shower.

13. C

Weightlessness due to the effect of microgravity causes many complications but not extra weight gain. Bones and muscles have less pressure so they expand. Astronauts experience a loss of bone tissue, which leads to backaches. Body fluid migration from the heart toward the brain leads to blocked sinuses. Red blood cell count falls, which leads to anemia. All these conditions are due to microgravity.

14. A

In multistage rockets, the successive discarding of the stages is done in order to reduce the weight of the fuselage and increase the mass to ratio of the rocket. It is an efficient method of increasing the speed of the rocket.

15. C

Ion drives use xenon gas instead of chemical fuels, but solar sails use the electromagnetic energy of the sun in the form of photons. Solar energy is transmitted into motion.

16. A

Space shuttles are also used in returning previously deployed satellites to Earth. Telescopes are used to observe celestial bodies, cameras are used to take photographs, and weather forecasting is done by Earth-orbiting satellites.

17. B

Landsat and RADARSAT are two Canadian satellites that are used to follow ships, monitor soil quality, track forest fires, and search for natural resources. They are not in geosynchronous orbit.

18. C

To receive the continuous signals for television communication and direct broadcast, a satellite is placed in a geostationary orbit. In this type of orbit, the satellite remains over the same spot on Earth's equator. Satellites in geostationary orbit enable long-distance voice, data, and television communication, to occur.

19. D

The Hubble Space Telescope has provided the best available view of a collision of Jupiter and Shoemaker Levy 9 in 1994. It has also provided evidence of the existence of black holes.

20. C

Optical interferometry is used to improve the resdution of images. To achieve this, signals from several telescopes in different locations are combined into one image.

NR 1   4213

A reflecting telescope uses a large primary mirror and a smaller secondary mirror to enlarge the image.

NR 2   2134

The solar sail allows space vehicles to use sunlight to propel themselves. The ion drive is a type of engine that uses cost-effective xenon gas as fuel. A space probe is a spacecraft that can carry out robotic exploration. A space station is considered to be an orbiting space community.

1.   *List four hazards associated with survival in space.*

These are some of the possible hazards associated with survival in space:

1. Psychological problems associated with being confined in a small space

2. Exposure to high levels of radiation

3. Dangers associated with floating space junk

4. Physical strain on the body

5. Problems associated with weightlessness

2.   *Compare the heliocentric and geocentric models of the solar system.*

The geocentric model was proposed by Aristotle about 2 000 years ago. It stated that Earth was the centre of the solar system and all planets revolved around Earth.

Copernicus proposed the heliocentric model in the 1500s. He stated that the sun was the centre of the solar system and all planets revolved around the sun.

3.   *A car is stuck in a remote rural area, but luckily it has a GPS system. Explain what GPS is and how it works to locate the stranded vehicle.*

GPS or global positioning system works by sending signals to satellites.

A built-in receiver sends signals to a minimum of three orbiting satellites. From the satellite signals, a computer calculation can pinpoint the exact location of the stranded vehicle in relation to the location of the satellites.

NOTES

KEY Strategies for Success on Tests

KEY STRATEGIES FOR SUCCESS ON TESTS

AN OVERVIEW OF THE TEST

This section is all about the skills and strategies you need to be successful on the Alberta Science 9 Provincial Achievement Test. It is designed for you to use together with your classroom learning and assignments.

Finding Out About the Test

Here are some questions you may wish to discuss with your teacher to help you prepare for the Alberta Science 9 Provincial Achievement Test.

1.	What will this test assess?	The test assesses the expectations from the five course topics: Biological Diversity, Matter and Chemical Change, Environmental Chemistry, Electrical Principles and Technologies, and Space Exploration. The questions will test your ability to understand and apply the scientific concepts you have learned throughout the year.
2.	What materials do I need to bring to write the test?	You need a pencil, an eraser, and a calculator.
3.	Can I use a calculator during the test?	Yes, you are allowed to use a calculator.
4.	Are there any materials provided for the test?	Data pages containing references such as the periodic table will be provided with the exam.
5.	What kinds of questions are on the test?	The test consists of 50 multiple choice questions and 5 numerical-response questions, electricity formulas, etc., for a total of 55 questions.
6.	How much time do I have to write the test?	You will have 75 minutes, plus 30 minutes of additional time to complete the examination.
7.	How important is this test to my final grade?	Your teacher can answer this question.
8.	How many questions will be on each content strand?	The Process of Science Strand is integrated into the questions for the other strands. The breakdown of questions will be approximately: 20% Biological Diversity, 20% Matter and Chemical Change, 20% Environmental Chemistry, 20% Electrical Principles and Technologies, and 20% Space Exploration.

Having an understanding of effective test-taking skills can help your performance on the test. Being familiar with the question formats may help you to prepare for quizzes, unit tests, and year-end assessments.

TEST PREPARATION AND TEST-TAKING SKILLS

THINGS TO CONSIDER WHEN TAKING A TEST

- It is normal to feel anxious before you write a test. You can manage this anxiety by:
  - Thinking positive thoughts. Imagine yourself doing well on the test.
  - Making a conscious effort to relax by taking several slow, deep, controlled breaths. Concentrate on the air going in and out of your body.
- Before you begin the test, ask questions if you are unsure of anything.
- Jot down key words or phrases from any instructions your teacher gives you.
- Look over the entire test to find out the number and kinds of questions on the test.
- Read each question closely and reread if necessary.
- Pay close attention to key vocabulary words. Sometimes these are **bolded** or *italicized*, and they are usually important words in the question.
- If you are putting your answers on an answer sheet, mark your answers carefully. Always print clearly. If you wish to change an answer, erase the mark completely and then ensure your final answer is darker than the one you have erased.
- Use highlighting to note directions, key words, and vocabulary that you find confusing or that are important to answering the question.
- Double-check to make sure you have answered everything before handing in your test.

When taking tests, students often overlook the easy words. Failure to pay close attention to these words can result in an incorrect answer. One way to avoid this is to be aware of these words and to underline, circle, or highlight them while you are taking the test.

Even though some words are easy to understand, they can change the meaning of the entire question, so it is important that you pay attention to them. Here are some examples:

all	always	most likely	probably	best	not
difference	usually	except	most	unlikely	likely

1. Which of the following equations is **not** considered abiotic?

   A. wind

   B. bacteria

   C. sunlight

   D. precipitation

HELPFUL STRATEGIES FOR ANSWERING MULTIPLE-CHOICE QUESTIONS

A multiple-choice question gives you some information, and then asks you to select an answer from four choices. Each question has one correct answer. The other answers are distractors, which are incorrect. Below are some strategies to help you when answering multiple-choice questions.

- Quickly skim through the entire test. Find out how many questions there are and plan your time accordingly.

- Read and reread questions carefully. Underline key words and try to think of an answer before looking at the choices.

- If there is a graphic, look at the graphic, read the question, and go back to the graphic. Then, you may want to underline the important information from the question.

- Carefully read the choices. Read the question first and then each answer that goes with it.

- When choosing an answer, try to eliminate those choices that are clearly wrong or do not make sense.

- Some questions may ask you to select the best answer. These questions will always include words like *best*, *most appropriate*, or *most likely*. All of the answers will be correct to some degree, but one of the choices will be better than the others in some way. Carefully read all four choices before choosing the answer you think is the best.

- If you do not know the answer, or if the question does not make sense to you, it is better to guess than to leave it blank.

- Do not spend too much time on any one question. Make a mark (*) beside a difficult question and come back to it later. If you are leaving a question to come back to later, make sure you also leave the space on the answer sheet, if you are using one.

- Remember to go back to the difficult questions at the end of the test; sometimes clues are given throughout the test that will provide you with answers.

- Note any negative words like *no* or *not* and be sure your choice fits the question.

- Before changing an answer, be sure you have a very good reason to do so.

- Do not look for patterns on your answer sheet, if you are using one.

HELPFUL STRATEGIES FOR ANSWERING OPEN-RESPONSE QUESTIONS

A written response requires you to respond to a question or directive such as **explain**, **predict**, **list**, **describe**, **show your work**, **solve**, or **calculate.** In preparing for open-response tasks you may wish to:

- Read and reread the question carefully.
- Recognize and pay close attention to directing words such as *explain*, *show your work*, and *describe*.
- Underline key words and phrases that indicate what is required in your answer, such as *explain*, *estimate*, *answer*, *calculate*, or *show your work*.
- Write down rough, point-form notes regarding the information you want to include in your answer.
- Think about what you want to say and organize information and ideas in a coherent and concise manner within the time limit you have for the question.
- Be sure to answer every part of the question that is asked.
- Include as much information as you can when you are asked to explain your thinking.
- Include a picture or diagram if it will help to explain your thinking.
- Try to put your final answer to a problem in a complete sentence to be sure it is reasonable.
- Reread your response to ensure you have answered the question.
- Think: Does your answer make sense?
- Listen: Does it sound right?
- Use appropriate subject vocabulary and terms in your response.

ABOUT SCIENCE TESTS

What You Need to Know about Science Tests

To do well on a science test, you need to understand and apply your knowledge of scientific concepts. Reading skills can also make a difference in how well you perform. Reading skills can help you follow instructions and find key words, as well as read graphs, diagrams, and tables.

Science tests usually have two types of questions: knowledge questions and skill questions. Knowledge questions test for your understanding of science ideas. Skill questions test how you would use your science knowledge.

How You Can Prepare for Science Tests

Below are some strategies that are particular to preparing for and writing science tests.

- Note-taking is a good way to review and study important information from your class notes and textbook.

- Sketch a picture of the process or idea being described in a question. Drawing is helpful for learning and remembering concepts.

- Check your answer to practice questions the require formulas by working backward to the beginning. You can find the beginning by going step-by-step in reverse order.

- When answering questions with graphics (pictures, diagrams, tables, or graphs), read the test question carefully.

  - Read the title of the graphic and any key words.

  - Read the test question carefully to figure out what information you need to find in the graphic.

  - Go back to the graphic to find the information you need.

- Always pay close attention when pressing the keys on your calculator. Repeat the procedure a second time to be sure you pressed the correct keys.

TEST PREPARATION COUNTDOWN

If you develop a plan for studying and test preparation, you will perform well on tests.

Here is a general plan to follow seven days before you write a test.

Countdown: 7 Days before the Test

1. Use "Finding Out About the Test" to help you make your own personal test preparation plan.

2. Review the following information:
   – Areas to be included on the test

   – Types of test items

   – General and specific test tips

3. Start preparing for the test at least 7 days before the test. Develop your test preparation plan and set time aside to prepare and study.

Countdown: 6, 5, 4, 3, 2 Days before the Test

1. Review old homework assignments, quizzes, and tests.

2. Rework problems on quizzes and tests to make sure you still know how to solve them.

3. Correct any errors made on quizzes and tests.

4. Review key concepts, processes, formulas, and vocabulary.

5. Create practice test questions for yourself and then answer them. Work out many sample problems.

Countdown: The Night before the Test

1. The night before the test is for final preparation, which includes reviewing and gathering material needed for the test before going to bed.

2. Most important is getting a good night's rest and knowing you have done everything possible to do well on the test.

Test Day

1. Eat a healthy and nutritious breakfast.

2. Ensure you have all the necessary materials.

3. Think positive thoughts: "I can do this." "I am ready." "I know I can do well."

4. Arrive at your school early so you are not rushing, which can cause you anxiety and stress.

SUMMARY OF HOW TO BE SUCCESSFUL DURING A TEST

You may find some of the following strategies useful for writing a test.

- Take two or three deep breaths to help you relax.
- Read the directions carefully and underline, circle, or highlight any important words.
- Look over the entire test to understand what you will need to do.
- Budget your time.
- Begin with an easy question, or a question you know you can answer correctly, rather than following the numerical question order of the test.
- If you cannot remember how to answer a question, try repeating the deep breathing and physical relaxation activities first. Then, move on to visualization and positive self-talk to get yourself going.
- When answering a question with graphics (pictures, diagrams, tables, or graphs), look at the question carefully.
  - Read the title of the graphic and any key words.
  - Read the test question carefully to figure out what information you need to find in the graphic.
  - Go back to the graphic to find the information you need.
- Write down anything you remember about the subject on the reverse side of your test paper. This activity sometimes helps to remind you that you do know something and you are capable of writing the test.
- Look over your test when you have finished and double-check your answers to be sure you did not forget anything.

A GUIDE TO WRITING THE PROVINCIAL ACHIEVEMENT TEST

The Provincial Achievement Test section contains all of the questions from the 2006 Achievement Test. It is recommended that students work carefully through these exams as they are reflective of the format and difficulty level of the final exam that students are likely to encounter.

2006 PROVINCIAL ACHIEVEMENT TEST

1. A sperm cell has the same number of chromosomes as

   A. an egg cell

   B. an embryo

   C. a blood cell

   D. a zygote

2. Scientists can insert a particular gene into corn kernels in order to protect corn against insect pests. This procedure is an example of

   A. artificial selection

   B. artificial insemination

   C. selective breeding

   D. genetic engineering

Use the following illustration to answer question 3.

3. Which of the following biological processes is **best** represented by the illustration above?

   A. Meiosis

   B. Budding

   C. Binary fission

   D. Spore production

Use the following information to answer question 4.

Characteristics of an Unknown Organism

• Has its niche at the surface of the soil

• Uses water and minerals from the soil

• Supplies food and oxygen to other organisms

4. Given the characteristics listed above, the unknown organism could be a

   A. clover

   B. mushroom

   C. virus

   D. worm

Use the following information to answer question 5.

Reproductive Characteristics of a Particular Species

• Able to reproduce once a year only

• Able to produce two offspring each time it reproduces

• Genetic information transferred to the offspring during reproduction

• One or two zygotes formed in the reproductive process

5. Which of the following statements correctly describes the reproductive process of this species?

   A. Reproduction is sexual because genetic information is transferred to the offspring only from the female.

   B. Reproduction is sexual because a zygote is formed.

   C. Reproduction is asexual because few offspring are produced at one time.

   D. Reproduction is asexual because the species might only have an offspring every six months.

Use the following information to answer questions 6 and 7.

1. Corn plants with desirable characteristics are identified within a crop. Only seeds from these plants are used to grow next year's crop.

2. Cells taken from a pea plant with desirable characteristics are reproduced in a Petri dish that contains nutrients necessary for growth.

3. Embryos are produced from the sperm and eggs of a prize bull and cow. These embryos are implanted into other cows.

4. Human genes are inserted into the fertilized eggs of cows.

6. Which biotechnology practice listed above has the **longest** history of use?

   A. 1

   B. 2

   C. 3

   D. 4

7. THIS TEST ITEM WAS DELETED IN 2006.

Use the following information to answer question 8.

Information About Malaria

- Malaria, a serious disease, is caused by a parasite that is spread by the bite of an infected mosquito.

- People travelling in areas where there is a high risk of contracting malaria used to be prescribed chloroquine pills to prevent the disease.

- Now, other treatments are usually prescribed because chloroquine is no longer guaranteed to be effective.

8. The **most probable** reason that chloroquine is less effective than it used to be in preventing the onset of malaria is that

   A. malaria parasites have developed a resistance to chloroquine

   B. mosquitoes have developed a resistance to the malaria parasite

   C. people have developed a resistance to chloroquine

   D. people have developed a resistance to the malaria parasite

Use the following information to answer question 9.

Statements About Different Species	
Statement I	Passenger pigeons were overhunted.
Statement II	Grizzly bears are no longer found in Mexico.
Statement III	Panda bears rely mainly on one food source.
Statement IV	Northern cod stocks off the coast of Newfoundland have been reduced.

9. Which of the statements above describes a species that has undergone extirpation?

   A. I

   B. II

   C. III

   D. IV

Use the following table to answer question 10.

Characteristics of Five Students

Student	Swimming Ability	Tongue-Rolling Ability	Skin Colour	Earlobe Shape
I	yes	no	light brown	hanging
II	yes	yes	light brown	hanging
III	no	yes	white	attached
IV	yes	yes	dark brown	hanging
V	no	no	white	attached

10. Which of the following pairs of students share a characteristic that is not a heritable trait?

 A. Students I and III

 B. Students I and V

 C. Students II and III

 D. Students II and IV

Use the following information to answer numerical-response question 1.

White-tailed jackrabbits live on the prairies,
          1   2

are consumers, and have fur that changes colour
     3   4

with the seasons.

Numerical Response

1. Match each of the underlined words numbered above to the term below that relates to it. Use each number only once.

 Ecosystem   ___ ___
 Niche   ___ ___
 Species   ___ ___
 Adaptation   ___ ___
 (Record your answer as a **four-digit** number.)

Use the following equation to answer question 11.

$$Mg_{(s)} + CuO_{(s)} \rightarrow MgO_{(s)} + Cu_{(s)}$$

11. Which of the following word equations correctly restates the equation above?

 A. Magnesium + copper
 $\rightarrow$ magnesium oxide + copper(II) oxide

 B. Magnesium + copper
 $\rightarrow$ magnesium oxide + oxide copper(II)

 C. Magnesium + copper(II) oxide
 $\rightarrow$ magnesium oxide + copper

 D. Magnesium + oxide copper(II)
 $\rightarrow$ magnesium oxide + copper

Use the following diagram to answer question 12.

Carbon Tetrahydride (Methane)

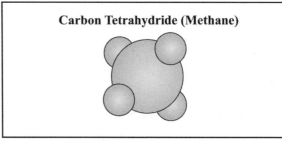

12. The chemical formula for the molecular compound shown above is

 A. C_4H

 B. CH_4

 C. C_4H_3

 D. C_3H_4

Use the following table to answer question 13.

Observations from Four Experiments That Involve Mixtures

Experiment	Procedure	Observation
I	White powder is added to water.	Gas is given off.
II	A solution is heated until it boils.	Vapour rises, and solute is left in the beaker.
III	Yellow powder is added to water.	Powder dissolves.
IV	A pure solution is added to another pure solution.	A powder appears at the bottom of the beaker.

13. In which two of the experiments above did a physical change occur?
   A. I and III
   B. I and IV
   C. II and III
   D. II and IV

14. The chemical formula for iron(II) chloride is $FeCl_2$. The total number of atoms in one molecule of iron(II) chloride is
   A. 1
   B. 2
   C. 3
   D. 4

Use the following excerpt from the periodic table to answer questions 15 to 18.

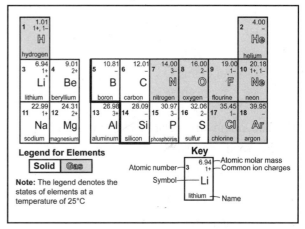

15. Which of the following statements presents correct information about an element in the excerpt from the periodic table shown above?
   A. Fluorine atoms can have 6 protons.
   B. Carbon atoms can have 20 protons.
   C. Sodium atoms can have 16 protons.
   D. Phosphorus atoms can have 15 protons.

16. Which of the following elements is the least reactive?
   A. Chlorine
   B. Sodium
   C. Argon
   D. Boron

17. When solid LiF is added to water, the resulting solution is
   A. molecular and does not conduct electricity
   B. ionic and does not conduct electricity
   C. molecular and conducts electricity
   D. ionic and conducts electricity

Use the following additional information to answer question 18.

A Chemical Reaction

$$Fe_{(s)} + \frac{?}{?} \rightarrow FeO_{(s)}$$
$$56 \text{ grams} \qquad 72 \text{ grams}$$

---

18. The unknown reactant and its mass are

A. oxide and 16 g

B. oxide and 128 g

C. oxygen and 16 g

D. oxygen and 128 g

Use the following information to answer question 19.

A teacher demonstrated a procedure to dilute a concentrated acid. The temperature of the reactants was 20 °C, and the temperature of the products was 75 °C.

---

19. Which of the following rows identifies the type of reaction that occurred in the procedure and the change in the temperature of the solution?

Row	Type of Reaction	Temperature Change
A.	Exothermic	Increase
B.	Exothermic	Decrease
C.	Endothermic	Increase
D.	Endothermic	Decrease

Use the following information to answer question 20.

In an experiment, a student immerses four nails composed of different metals in a dilute corrosive solution. Each nail has the same surface area. The student measures the mass of each nail before the experiment and then again after the nail has been immersed in the corrosive solution for 20 minutes. The results are recorded in the table below.

Type of Metal Nail	Mass of Nail (g)	
	Before	After
Metal W	1.1	0.6
Metal X	1.3	0.7
Metal Y	1.5	1.2
Metal Z	1.8	1.4

---

20. According to the information above, the metal that would react most readily to a dilute corrosive solution is

A. Metal W

B. Metal X

C. Metal Y

D. Metal Z

Use the following information to answer question 21.

A researcher hypothesized that ultraviolet radiation prevents pigeon eggs from hatching. To test this hypothesis, the researcher divided fertilized pigeon eggs into six groups. During incubation, five of the groups were exposed to different intensities of ultraviolet radiation for 24 hours, but the sixth group was not. The number of eggs that hatched in each group was recorded.

---

21. What is the responding variable in this experiment?

    A. Intensity of ultraviolet radiation

    B. Amount of time exposed to ultraviolet radiation

    C. Group of eggs not exposed to ultraviolet radiation

    D. Number of eggs that hatched after exposure to ultraviolet radiation

Use the following diagram to answer numerical-response question 2.

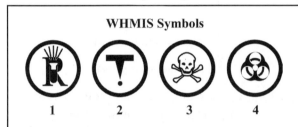

WHMIS Symbols

1   2   3   4

Numerical Reponse

2. Match each WHMIS symbol above with its corresponding description, as given below. Use each number only once.

WHMIS Symbol: ___   ___   ___   ___

| Description: | Poisonous and infectious material causing immediate and serious toxic effects | Biohazardous infectious material | Dangerously reactive material | Poisonous and infectious material causing other toxic effects |

(Record your answer as a **four-digit** number.)

22. The process by which toxins are concentrated as they move up the food chain is called

    A. pollution

    B. biomagnification

    C. web magnification

    D. biomass stratification

Use the following graph to answer question 23.

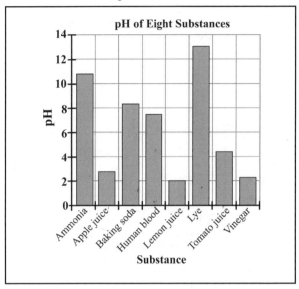

23. Which of the following conclusions can be made from the graph above?

    A. Vinegar is more basic than lye.

    B. Ammonia is more acidic than apple juice.

    C. Baking soda is more basic than human blood.

    D. Tomato juice is more acidic than lemon juice.

24. Which of the following statements describes one characteristic shared by **all** biodegradable substances?

    A. They can be broken down by inorganic compounds.

    B. They can be broken down by simple organisms.

    C. They decompose faster at low temperatures.

    D. They decompose faster in dry conditions.

Use the following graph to answer question 25.

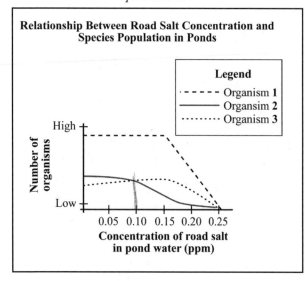

Relationship Between Road Salt Concentration and Species Population in Ponds

Legend
- - - - - Organism **1**
———— Organsim **2**
·········· Organism **3**

25. According to the graph above, an increase in the concentration of road salt in pond water from zero to 0.10 ppm results in a decrease in the number of

A. organism 1

B. organism 2

C. organisms 1 and 3

D. organisms 2 and 3

26. Water in a particular lake has a pH of 5.2. Calcium carbonate is added to the lake water. The purpose of treating the lake water with calcium carbonate is to

A. decrease the basic nature of the lake water

B. increase the acidic nature of the lake water

C. bring the pH of the lake water closer to 7.0

D. bring the pH of the lake water closer to zero

Use the following information to answer questions 27 and 28.

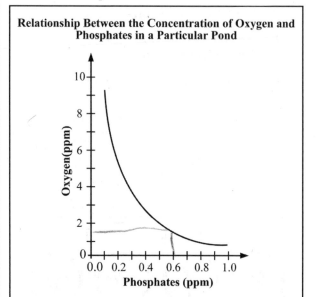

Relationship Between the Concentration of Oxygen and Phosphates in a Particular Pond

Minimum O_2 Concentrations Within Which Invertebrates Can Survive

O_2 Concentration (ppm)	Invertebrates
8–10	Stonefly nymph
4–8	Dragonfly nymph
0–4	Midge larvae

27. Which of the following statements describes the relationship between oxygen concentration and phosphate concentration that is illustrated in the graph?

A. As oxygen levels increase, phosphate levels increase.

B. As oxygen levels increase, phosphate levels stay the same.

C. As phosphate levels increase, oxygen levels decrease.

D. As phosphate levels increase, oxygen levels stay the same.

28. If a sample of water contains an abundance of dragonfly nymphs and no stonefly nymphs, then the phosphate level of the water **most likely** falls within which of the following phosphate ranges?

   A. 0.1–0.2 ppm

   B. 0.2–0.4 ppm

   C. 0.4–0.6 ppm

   D. 0.8–1.0 ppm

29. A dissolved oxygen concentration of 6 ppm indicates that 6 mL of oxygen is dissolved in

   A. 100 mL of water

   B. 1 000 mL of water

   C. 10 000 mL of water

   D. 1 000 000 mL of water

Use the following information to answer question 30.

Opinions Related to the Issue of Non-Renewable Resources

I "Companies must reduce the price of gasoline."

II "Citizens must be encouraged to use public transportation."

III "Tax incentives must be given to individuals to buy houses."

IV "Government must create incentives to develop alternative energy sources."

V "Legislation that requires energy-efficient cars must be put in place."

---

30. Which of the opinions given above refer to actions that promote long-term energy conservation?

   A. I, II, and III

   B. I, III, and IV

   C. II, III, and V

   D. II, IV, and V

Numerical Response

3. For each of the substances listed below, indicate whether it is organic or inorganic using the following code.

1 = Organic
2 = Inorganic

Potassium ____
Magnesium ____
Carbohydrate ____
Salt ____

(Record your answer as a **four-digit** number.)

31. The most common type of energy loss in electrical devices is

   A. thermal

   B. potential

   C. chemical

   D. mechanical

Use the following information to answer question 32.

A ride in an amusement park is controlled by an operator who turns a dial to make the seats rotate faster. As the operator turns the dial, more current flows to the motors.

---

32. Which of the following electrical devices causes the seats on the amusement park ride to rotate faster?

   A. Variable resistor

   B. Circuit breaker

   C. Generator

   D. Ammeter

Use the following information to answer questions 33 and 34.

Models that Represent Current, Voltage, and Resistance in Two Electrical Circuits

Model **1**   Model **2**

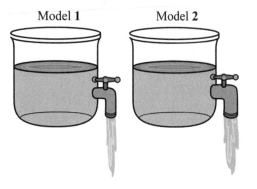

Components in the Models

I	The amount of water that flows from the spout
II	The force of gravity acting on the water
III	The amount of water in the jug
IV	The diameter of the spout

33. Which of the components in the models represents resistance in a DC circuit?

A. I

B. II

C. III

D. IV

34. Which of the components in the models represents current in a DC circuit?

A. I

B. II

C. III

D. IV

Use the following information to answer question 35.

Four Electrical Circuits

Circuit 1	1 battery, 3 light bulbs wired in series
Circuit 2	1 battery, 5 light bulbs wired in series
Circuit 3	1 battery, 3 light bulbs wired in parallel
Circuit 4	1 battery, 5 light bulbs wired in parallel

All of the light bulbs and batteries are identical.

35. When connected, which of the electrical circuits described above will result in the dimmest light?

A. Circuit 1

B. Circuit 2

C. Circuit 3

D. Circuit 4

36. Which of the following rows identifies the correct circuit distance, amperage, resistance, and control device of a working microelectronic circuit?

Row	Circuit Distance	Amperage	Resistance	Control Device
A.	Short	Low	Low	Transistor
B.	Short	High	High	Transistor
C.	Long	Low	Low	Switch
D.	Long	High	High	Switch

37. Which of the following parts of a lead storage car battery is acidic?

A. Electrode

B. Electrolyte

C. Positive terminal

D. Negative terminal

Use the following information to answer question 38.

Description of a Circuit	Legend
An electric pump is connected to a car battery. The speed of the pump is controlled by a dial.	‖⊪ Car battery ⊓ Electric pump ⋀ Resistor ⋀ Variable resistor ／ Ignition switch for car

38. Which of the following schematic diagrams **best** illustrates the circuit described above?

A.

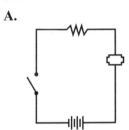

B.

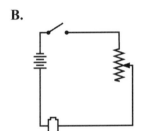

C.

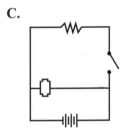

D.

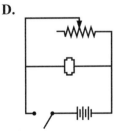

39. QUESTION 39 IS STILL SECURED AND WILL NOT BE RELEASED.

40. Which of the following actions will **not** reduce the energy used?

- **A.** Adding a layer of insulation to your refrigerator
- **B.** Replacing incandescent bulbs with fluorescent bulbs
- **C.** Washing clothes in cold water rather than in hot water
- **D.** Watching television in the afternoon rather than in the early evening

Use the following information to answer numerical-response question 4.

Types of Power Generation	
1. Coal-fired	2. Hydroelectric
3. Nuclear	4. Solar

Numerical Response

4. Match each type of power generation listed above with one of its disadvantages, given below.

Disrupts the movement of aquatic organisms _____

Emits carbon dioxide and sulfur dioxide into the air _____

Is an inconsistent method of power generation _____

Requires the long-term storage of hazardous waste products _____

(Record your answer as a **four-digit** number.)

41. Models of the universe that place Earth at the centre are described as

    A. heliocentric models

    B. astronomic models

    C. geocentric models

    D. galactic models

42. The orbit that Earth makes around the sun is **best** described as

    A. circular

    B. celestial

    C. elliptical

    D. gravitational

43. Which of the following graphs correctly represents the relationship between the orbit times of planets and their distance from the sun?

A.

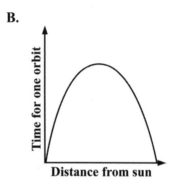

B.

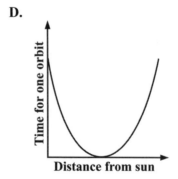

C.

D.

44. Mars is visible on a clear night because it

A. reflects light

B. refracts light

C. absorbs light

D. produces light

45. Triangulation is the measurement process that astronomers use to estimate the

A. size of a celestial body

B. orbit of a celestial body

C. distance to a celestial body from Earth

D. angle between a celestial body and Earth

Use the following information to answer question 46.

True and False Statements About Refracting Telescopes	
Statement 1	Refracting telescopes use mirrors.
Statement 2	Refracting telescopes were the first type to be designed.
Statement 3	The image from a refracting telescope is not distorted by atmospheric interference.
Statement 4	A refracting telescope has an eyepiece and an objective lens.

46. Which of the statements above are **true**?

A. Statements 1 and 3

B. Statements 1 and 4

C. Statements 2 and 3

D. Statements 2 and 4

47. A celestial object that is located 10° above the horizon in the northeast part of the sky has an

A. azimuth of 45° and an altitude of 10°

B. azimuth of 10° and an altitude of 45°

C. azimuth of 315° and an altitude of 10°

D. azimuth of 10° and an altitude of 315°

48. For a particular satellite to provide an uninterrupted television signal to a particular viewer 24 hours a day and seven days a week, it must

A. travel in a low Earth orbit

B. travel in a geosynchronous orbit

C. be a remote-sensing satellite

D. be a Global Positioning System satellite

49. Most of the outer planets of our solar system are

A. gaseous, small, and have few moons

B. gaseous, large, and have many moons

C. terrestrial, small, and have few moons

D. terrestrial, large, and have many moons

Use the following diagram to answer question 50.

Spectrum of Visible Light

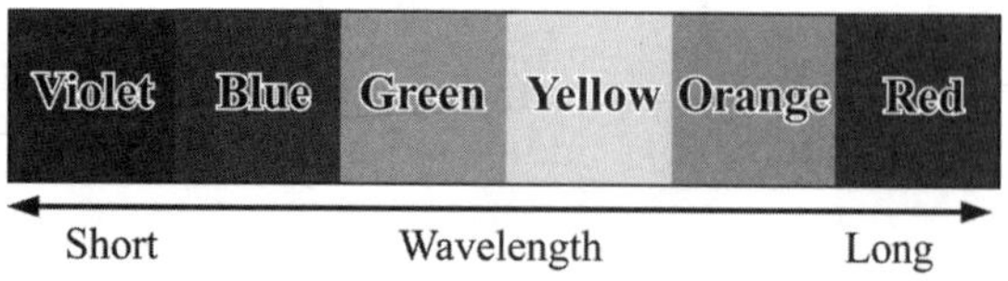

| Violet | Blue | Green | Yellow | Orange | Red |

Short ← Wavelength → Long

50. Which of the following descriptions identifies a red-shifted star?

A. A star that is larger than Earth

B. A star that is smaller than Earth

C. A star that is moving toward Earth

D. A star that is moving away from Earth

Use the following information to answer numerical-response question 5.

Four Parts of the Universe

1. Solar system   2. Milky Way

3. Jupiter   4. The moon

Numerical Response

5. List the parts of the universe given above in order from the part with the smallest mass to the part with the greatest mass.

____,   ____,   ____,   and   ____.
Smallest   **Greatest**
mass   **mass**

(Record your answer as a **four-digit** number.)

ANSWERS AND SOLUTIONS—2006 PROVINCIAL
ACHIEVEMENT TEST

1. A	11. C	NR2. 3412	31. A	41. C
2. D	12. B	22. B	32. A	42. C
3. C	13. C	23. C	33. D	43. C
4. A	14. C	24. B	34. A	44. A
5. B	15. D	25. B	35. B	45. C
6. A	16. C	26. C	36. A	46. D
7. OMITTED	17. D	27. C	37. B	47. A
8. A	18. C	28. B	38. B	48. B
9. B	19. A	29. D	39. OMITTED	49. B
10. D	20. B	30. D	40. D	50. D
NR1. 2314	21. D	NR3. 2212	NR4. 2143	NR5. 4312

1. A

Sperm and egg cells are both gametes.
Gametes have half the number of chromosomes of other cells. Gametes have 23 chromosomes while somatic (body) cells have 46 chromosomes.

2. D

When a foreign gene is inserted into an organism, it is known as genetic engineering. Artificial selection and artificial insemination select for desirable traits, but they do so by picking traits that are already present in the organism, not by inserting new DNA.

3. C

The diagram shows a cell dividing once into two identical daughter cells. This process is called binary fission. Meiosis involves two divisions and results in four haploid cells. Budding and spore production are other methods of asexual reproduction, but they do not involve the splitting of one cell into two identical cells.

4. A

A clover lives at the surface of the soil. It uses water and minerals from the soil and photosynthesizes, producing oxygen for other organisms to use. A clover is also a food source for certain animals. Worms live beneath the soil. Viruses do not supply either oxygen or food for other organisms. Mushrooms do not supply oxygen to other animals, because they are fungi that do not photosynthesize.

5. B

Sexual reproduction results in genetic information being transferred from the male and the female parent to the offspring. After the fertilization of the egg by the sperm, a zygote is formed. This process is more time consuming than asexual reproduction and results in relatively few offspring. Asexual reproduction produces a large number of genetically identical offspring in a short period of time.

6. A

Identifying desirable characteristics in corn crops and saving the best seeds to plant the next year is known as artificial selection. This agricultural practice has existed for roughly 10 000 years. Cloning, artificial insemination, and genetic engineering are all technologies from the 20th century.

7. OMITTED

8. A

Because of genetic mutations, natural selection can occur. According to natural selection, members of a species that exhibit certain characteristics will be able to survive when the environment changes. In this case, a species of parasite that causes malaria has developed a resistance to the drug chloroquine. This means that the drug is no longer able to kill the parasite and other treatments must be used.

9. B

Extirpation refers to the complete disappearance of a species from a particular area and is sometimes referred to as local extinction. The grizzly bear's disappearance from Mexico is an example of extirpation. Passenger pigeons are extinct and not extirpated. The presence of some cod off the coast of Newfoundland means they are not extirpated. The panda bear's one food source is the reason they are considered a highly specialized species, but it does not mean they are extirpated.

10. D

Heritable traits are passed down from parents to offspring by genetic material (DNA). Tongue-rolling ability, skin colour, and earlobe shape are all examples of heritable traits. The only characteristic listed that is not heritable is swimming ability. Students II and IV are the only pair listed that share this characteristic.

NR 1   2314

The white-tailed jackrabbit is a species of rabbit that lives in a prairie ecosystem. They are consumers in their ecosystem, or niche. An example of an adaptation of the white-tailed jackrabbit is its ability to change fur colour with the seasons. This provides them with the ability to camouflage themselves from predators.

11. C

Magnesium reacts with copper(II) oxide to produce magnesium oxide and copper. When naming multivalent ionic compounds, the ion charge, in Roman numerals, must be placed behind the atom's name. Also, the name of the metal always comes first and is followed by the nonmetal.

12. B

According to its IUPAC name, carbon tetrahydride has one carbon atom and four hydrogen atoms, indicated by the prefix tetra-. The diagram illustrates a larger carbon atom bonded to four smaller hydrogen atoms. The proper chemical formula for this molecular compound is CH_4.

13. C

A physical change is one in which no new products are formed. The change is also reversible. Boiling a solution until the water evaporates and a solute is left at the bottom of the beaker is a physical change because the water can be collected and used to dissolve the solute again. State changes are also physical changes. Dissolving a solute, such as yellow powder, in water is a physical change. Evidence of a chemical change includes the formation of a gas, a colour change, the formation of a precipitate, a change in temperature, or an odour given off.

14. C

According to the chemical formula for iron(II) chloride, the molecule contains one iron atom and two chlorine atoms. Therefore, each molecule of $FeCl_2$ will contain three atoms in total.

15. D

The number of protons an element contains is equal to its number on the periodic table. Phosphorus has an atomic number of 15. This means phosphorus has 15 protons.

16. C

Of the elements listed, argon is the least reactive because it is a noble gas. Noble gases are considered inert because they do not bond with other elements to form compounds.

17. D

LiF is an ionic compound because it contains both a metal and a nonmetal. When it is dissolved in water, it will result in an ionic solution.
Ionic compounds in solution conduct electricity.

18. C

Iron reacts with oxygen to produce iron(II) oxide. An element by itself does not have the –ide ending. According to the law of conservation of mass, the mass of the reactants must equal the mass of the products. Because the mass of the product is 72 g, the mass of the reactants needs to be 72 g. To find the mass of oxygen, subtract the mass of iron from the mass of the product.

72 g – 56 = 16 g of oxygen

19. A

Since the temperature of the products was higher than that of the reactants in this reaction, it gave off heat. A reaction that gives off heat and results in an increase in temperature is exothermic.

20. B

The metal that reacts most readily to a dilute corrosive solution will show the most corrosion. This is determined by measuring the change of the mass of each nail. To calculate which metal nail changed the most, the difference between the initial mass and the final mass must be found.

Type of Metal Nail	Mass of Nail (g)		
	Before	After	Difference (Before – After)
Metal W	1.1	0.6	0.5
Metal X	1.3	0.7	0.6
Metal Y	1.5	1.2	0.3
Metal Z	1.8	1.4	0.4

The mass of the nail made of metal X changed the most due to corrosion. Therefore, metal X reacts most readily with dilute corrosive solutions.

21. D

The responding variable is the variable measured in the experiment. In this case, the quantity measured was the number of eggs that hatched as a result of the exposure to UV radiation. The intensity of the UV radiation was the manipulated variable, and the controls for the experiment were the time of exposure and the group that was not exposed to any amount of UV radiation.

The diagram summarizes each of the WHMIS symbols.

Compressed Gas   Flammable and Combustible Material   Oxidizing Material   Poisonous Materials Causing Immediate and Serious Toxic Effects

Materials Causing Other Toxic Effects   Biohazardous Infectious Material   Corrosive Material   Dangerously Reactive Material

Therefore, symbol 1 represents dangerously reactive material, symbol 2 represents poisonous and infectious material causing other toxic effects, symbol 3 represents poisonous and infectious material causing immediate and serious toxic effects, and symbol 4 represents biohazardous infectious material.

22. B

Biomagnification is the increase in the concentration of toxins as they move up trophic levels. The last animal in the food chain will consume the highest concentration of toxins because these toxins have been amplified through the chain. An example of biomagnification is the increasing concentration of mercury in fish that are found in higher levels of the food chain.

23. C

pH is a measure of the hydrogen ions in a substance. A pH less than 7 indicates an acid and a pH greater than 7 indicates a base. A neutral substance has a pH of 7. From the graph, it can be concluded that baking soda is more basic than human blood because it has a higher pH. The more basic a substance is, the higher its pH.

24. B

The term biodegradable refers to substances which can be broken down by simple organisms. Biodegradable substances are often organic. The decomposition rate of biodegradable substances can usually be increased by increasing the temperature or adding moisture to the environment.

25. B

According to the graph, when the road salt concentration of pond water increases from 0 ppm to 0.10 ppm, the only organism whose population decreases is organism 2. At this level of concentration, the population of organism 1 remains the same and the population of organism 3 increases slightly.

26. C

A pH less than 7 indicates that the lake is acidic. Calcium carbonate is a base that will increase the pH of the acidic lake water and bring it closer to 7.0. The reaction between an acid and a base is called a neutralization reaction. It can be represented by the equation
acid + base → water + salt.

27. C

The graph indicates that as phosphate levels increase, the oxygen levels in the pond decrease. For example, when the phosphate concentration is 0.1 ppm, the oxygen concentration is about 9 ppm. When the phosphate concentration increases to 0.4 ppm, the oxygen concentration decreases to 4 ppm.

28. B

According to the chart, dragonfly nymphs survive in an oxygen concentration range of 4-8 ppm. According to the graph, this oxygen concentration range corresponds to a phosphate concentration range of about 0.2-0.4 ppm.

29. D

Concentration can be measured in parts per million, or ppm. A concentration of 6 ppm means that 6 mL of oxygen is dissolved in 1 000 000 mL of water.

$$6 \text{ ppm} = \frac{6 \text{ mL}}{1\ 000\ 000 \text{ mL}}$$

30. D

Actions that promote long-term energy conservation focus on conserving resources and making more sustainable choices. The use of public transportation and the implementation of legislation requiring energy-efficient cars both reduce the amount of fossil fuels being used. Therefore, they conserve resources.
Offering incentives for the development of alternate energy sources is also a step toward energy conservation. Since the main sources of energy are non-renewable at the moment, alternative energy sources could help to conserve fossil fuels.

NR 3   2212

Organic substances contain carbon. Potassium and magnesium are pure elements and do not contain carbon. Carbohydrates are organic molecules made up of carbon, hydrogen, and oxygen. Salt, or sodium chloride, is made up of sodium and chlorine and does not contain carbon.

31. A

In energy transformations, the conversion is never 100% efficient, and some energy is always converted to a form that is not useful. The most common type of energy loss in electrical devices is thermal. This energy is lost as heat, which is produced as a result of friction. Because electrical devices have moving parts, friction is always present.

32. A

A variable resistor allows the operator to control the amount of current flowing to the motor. Variable resistors allow a change in current to occur gradually. To make the seats rotate faster in an amusement park, the operator needs to be able to gradually increase or decrease the speed of the motor. Therefore, the operator needs a variable resistor.

33. D

Resistance is a measure of how difficult it is for electrons to flow in a circuit. In the model, the component limiting how much water can flow out of the jug is the diameter of the spout. Therefore, the diameter of the spout represents resistance. The resistance of the larger spout is less because it is easier for more water to flow out of it. The smaller spout has a greater resistance because less water can flow through it at one time.

34. A

Current is the flow of electrons through a circuit. In the model, the water flowing through the spout represents the flow of electrons, or current. The force of gravity refers to potential difference, or voltage, and the diameter of the spout refers to resistance.

35. B

The lights on circuit 2 will be the dimmest because there are five bulbs, and they are all connected in series. Components connected in series increase the resistance of the circuit, which results in less current flowing. When less current is flowing, the bulbs are not as bright. When light bulbs are connected in parallel, the overall resistance of the circuit decreases, resulting in more brightly lit bulbs.

36. A

Microelectronic circuits, or microcircuits, have a very short circuit distance and use transistors instead of switches. There is little resistance in these circuits, and they have low amperage. They are found in electronic devices like computers and cellphones.

37. B

A lead storage car battery is an example of a wet cell. Wet cells have a liquid electrolyte, which is typically an acid. Lead storage car batteries use sulfuric acid as an electrolyte. The electrodes, one of which is the positive terminal while the other is the negative terminal, are two different metals.

38. B

The description specifies that an electric pump is connected to a battery and controlled by a dial. A dial is indicative of a variable resistor. With a variable resistor, the operator can gradually increase or decrease the resistance to the motor. In order for the pump to be controlled by the variable resistor, both the pump and the resistor must be connected in series. Diagram **B** shows this connection.

39. OMITTED

40. D

Watching television in the afternoon rather than in the evening will not reduce energy consumption. At any time of the day, the television uses the same amount of energy. Using cold water instead of hot water to wash clothes, using fluorescent light bulbs instead of incandescent light bulbs, and adding insulation to the refrigerator will all decrease the amount of energy consumed.

NR 4   2143

Hydroelectric energy can disrupt the habitat and movement of aquatic organisms because it relies on dams to harness energy. Coal-fired energy results in the release of carbon dioxide and sulfur dioxide into the air. Solar energy is unreliable because it is not available at night. Cloudy days can also interfere with the collection of solar energy. Nuclear energy produces hazardous waste products. These products must be properly stored in order to prevent them from harming people and the environment.

41. C

Earth-centred models of the universe are known as geocentric models. The current model of the solar system is heliocentric, meaning it is centred around the sun.

42. C

Johannes Kepler determined that planetary orbits are elliptical and not circular. Elliptical orbits better predict the movement of the planets. Kepler's theory is the current theory of planetary motion in the solar system.

43. C

The time it takes for planets to orbit the sun is directly proportional to their distance from the sun. This means that the farther a planet is from the sun, the longer it will take the planet to orbit the sun. For example, it takes Mercury only 88 days to orbit the sun once. It takes Earth 365 days to orbit the sun once. This is because Mercury is closer to the sun than Earth. Graph **C** correctly represents this relationship.

44. A

Mars is visible on a clear night because it reflects light from the sun toward Earth.

45. C

Triangulation is one way of obtaining the distance between a celestial body and Earth. It relies on the geometry of a triangle. By measuring the angles between the celestial body and a baseline from two different points, the distance to the body from Earth can be calculated.

46. D

Refracting telescopes were the first type of telescope to be designed. They use lenses, not mirrors, to magnify an object and have both an eyepiece and an objective lens. The image from a refracting telescope is distorted by atmospheric interference. Optics technology has been developed to help correct this distortion. Therefore, statements 2 and 4 are true.

47. A

The altitude refers to the height above the horizon and is measured in degrees. The information given in the question indicates that the altitude is 10°. Azimuth refers to the position relative to due north. Since the object is in the northeast quadrant of the sky, the azimuth angle must be between 0-90°. The coordinates matching this description are an azimuth of 45° and an altitude of 10°.

48. B

The satellite must be in a geosynchronous orbit to provide an uninterrupted signal. This means that it is moving at the same speed as Earth. This ensures that the satellite is always in the same position above Earth. Global Positioning System (GPS) and remote-sensing satellites are not in geosynchronous orbits because they need to provide information about more than one area of Earth.

49. B

The outer planets of the solar system are gaseous, large, and have many moons. They are referred to as Jovian because they are similar to Jupiter. In contrast, the four planets closest to the sun are rocky and small. They are called terrestrial because they are similar to Earth.

50. D

A red-shifted star is a star that is moving away from Earth. Light travels in waves, and the changes in wavelength can be used to determine the direction a star is moving. Wavelengths in front of a moving object are compressed while those behind it are spread out. This phenomenon is known as the Doppler effect. The wavelengths of light in front of a star are compressed if it is moving toward Earth. Shorter wavelengths of light are associated with the blue end of the spectrum. A shift toward the red end of the spectrum indicates longer wavelengths of light and means that the star is moving away from Earth.

NR 5   4312

Listed in order of increasing mass, from smallest to largest, the parts of the solar system are the moon, Jupiter, the solar system, and the Milky Way.

CREDITS

Every effort has been made to provide proper acknowledgement of the original source and to comply with copyright law. However, some attempts to establish original copyright ownership may have been unsuccessful. If copyright ownership can be identified, please notify Castle Rock Research Corp so that appropriate corrective action can be taken.

Some images in this document are from www.clipart.com, copyright (c) 2011 Jupiterimages Corporation.

ORDERING INFORMATION

SCHOOL ORDERS

Please contact the Learning Resource Centre (LRC) for school discount and order information.

THE KEY **Study Guides** are specifically designed to assist students in preparing for unit tests, final exams, and provincial examinations.

THE KEY **Study Guides** – $29.95 each plus G.S.T.

SENIOR HIGH		JUNIOR HIGH	ELEMENTARY
Biology 30	Biology 20	English Language Arts 9	English Language Arts 6
Chemistry 30	Chemistry 20	Math 9	Math 6
English 30-1	English 20-1	Science 9	Science 6
English 30-2	Mathematics 20-1	Social Studies 9	Social Studies 6
Applied Math 30	Physics 20	Math 8	Math 4
Pure Math 30	Social Studies 20-1	Math 7	English Language Arts 3
Physics 30	English 10-1		Math 3
Social Studies 30-1	Math 10 Combined		
Social Studies 30-2	Science 10		
	Social Studies 10-1		

Student Notes and Problems (SNAP) Workbooks contain complete explanations of curriculum concepts, examples, and exercise questions.

SNAP Workbooks – $29.95 each plus G.S.T.

SENIOR HIGH		JUNIOR HIGH	ELEMENTARY
Biology 30	Biology 20	Math 9	Math 6
Chemistry 30	Chemistry 20	Science 9	Math 5
Applied Math 30	Mathematics 20-1	Math 8	Math 4
Pure Math 30	Physics 20	Science 8	Math 3
Math 31	Math 10 Combined	Math 7	
Physics 30	Science 10	Science 7	

Visit our website for a tour of resource content and features or order resources online at
www.castlerockresearch.com

#2340, 10180 – 101 Street
Edmonton, AB Canada T5J 3S4
e-mail: learn@castlerockresearch.com

Phone: 780.448.9619
Toll-free: 1.800.840.6224
Fax: 780.426.3917

ORDER FORM

Learning Resources Centre

Learning Resources Centre

Castle Rock Research is pleased to announce an exclusive distribution arrangement with the Learning Resources Centre (LRC). Under this agreement, schools can now place all their orders with LRC for order fulfillment. As well, these resources are eligible for applying the Learning Resource Credit Allocation (LRCA), which gives schools a 25% discount off LRC's selling price. Call LRC for details.

Orders may be placed with LRC by
Telephone: 780.427.2767
Fax: 780.422.9750
Internet: www.lrc.education.gov.ab.ca
Or mail: 12360 – 142 Street NW
Edmonton, AB T5L 4X9

PAYMENT AND SHIPPING INFORMATION

Name: _____

School Telephone: _____

SHIP TO

School: _____

Address: _____

City: _____ Postal Code: _____

PAYMENT
☐ by credit card
VISA/MC Number: _____
Expiry Date: _____
Name on card: _____
☐ enclosed cheque
☐ invoice school   P.O. number: _____

THE KEY	QUANTITY
Biology 30	
Chemistry 30	
English 30-1	
English 30-2	
Applied Math 30	
Pure Math 30	
Physics 30	
Social Studies 30-1	
Social Studies 30-2	
Biology 20	
Chemistry 20	
Mathematics 20-1	
Physics 20	
Math 10 Combined	
Science 10	
Social Studies 10-1	
English Language Arts 9	
Math 9	
Science 9	
Social Studies 9	
Math 8	
Math 7	
English Language Arts 6	
Math 6	
Science 6	
Social Studies 6	
Math 4	
English Language Arts 3	
Math 3	

Student Notes and Problems Workbooks	QUANTITY	
	SNAP Workbooks	Solution Manuals
Math 31		
Biology 30		
Chemistry 30		
English 30-1		
English 30-2		
Applied Math 30		
Pure Math 30		
Physics 30		
Biology 20		
Chemistry 20		
Mathematics 20-1		
Physics 20		
Math 10 Combined		
Science 10		
English 20-1		
Mathematics 20-1		
Physics 20		
Social Studies 20-1		
English 10-1		
Math 10 Combined		
Science 10		
Social Studies 10-1		
English Language Arts 9		
Math 9		
Science 9		
Math 8		
Science 8		
Math 7		
Science 7		
Math 6		
Math 5		
Math 4		
Math 3		

TOTALS
KEYS
SNAP WORKBOOKS
SOLUTION MANUALS
SOLUTION MANUALS

#2340, 10180 – 101 Street, Edmonton, AB T5J 3S4   **Phone:** 780.448.9619 **Fax:** 780.426.3917
Email: learn@castlerockresearch.com   **Toll-free:** 1.800.840.6224

CASTLE ROCK
RESEARCH CORP

www.castlerockresearch.com